D0093595

MY OWN TWO FEET

BEVERLY CLEARY

MY OWN TWO FEET
A Memoir

AVON BOOKS  NEW YORK

The publisher and author gratefully acknowledge permission to reprint on page 84 "Music Goes Round and Round," by Ed Farley, Michael Riley, Red Hodgson, © 1935 Chappell & Co. (ASCAP) (renewed). All rights reserved. Used by permission of Warner Bros. Publications Inc., Miami, FL 33014

AVON BOOKS, INC.
1350 Avenue of the Americas
New York, New York 10019

First Avon Books Trade Paperback Printing: April 1999
First Avon Camelot Printing: October 1996

AVON TRADEMARK REG U S PAT OFF AND IN OTHER COUNTRIES, MARCA REGISTRADA, HECHO EN U S A

Printed in the U S A.

OPM 10 9 8 7 6 5 4 3

Contents

PART II: CHILDREN, CUSTOMERS, SOLDIERS

PART ONE

Friends,
Hopes,
Exams

Bus Trip to a New Life

The three of us, Mother, Dad, and I, stood on the sidewalk outside the Greyhound bus station in Portland, Oregon, searching for words we could not find or holding back words we could not speak. The sun, bronze from the smoke of September forest fires, cast an illusory light. Nothing seemed real, but it was. I was leaving, actually leaving, for California, the Golden State, land of poppies, big red geraniums, trees heavy with oranges, palm trees beneath cloudless skies, and best of all, no Depression. I had seen it all on postcards and in the movies, and so had the rest of my class at Grant High School. California was the goal of many. John Steinbeck had not yet, in 1934, revised our thinking.

3

And now I was one of the lucky ones going to this glorious place where people made movies all day and danced the night away. I was escaping the clatter of typewriters in business school and going instead to college. As I stood there in the smoky light in my neat navy blue dress, which Mother had measured a fashionable twelve inches from the floor when I made it, and with a five-dollar bill given to me by my father for emergencies rolled in my stocking, I tried to hide my elation from my parents.

Dad, I know, was sad to see his only child leave home, but the decision had been his. He had thoughtfully smoked his pipe for several evenings, mulling over the unexpected letter from Mother's cousin Verna Clapp inviting me to spend the winter with her family in Ontario in Southern California. I could attend tuition-free Chaffey Junior College, where she was the librarian.

Mother had dismissed the letter, saying, "Isn't that just like Verna, so impractical." The Depression had made Oregonians relentlessly practical. Dad, however, did not dismiss the letter. Finally, after he rapped his pipe against his ashtray, he said, "Beverly is going." Dad, a quiet man, had watched tension build between Mother and me as I resisted her struggles to mold me into her

4

ideal of a perfect daughter. He had also observed my increasing unhappiness over an obsessive young man I shall call Gerhart, six years older than I, whom I had come to dislike but who was unshakable because Mother encouraged him. "Now, you be nice to Gerhart," Mother often said. "He's a good boy, and he's lonely." Mother longed to have me popular with boys. Although I liked boys and was friendly with them at school, I was not concerned with popularity. As the months wore on, I wasn't at all nice to Gerhart. I was horrid.

At first Mother thought Dad's pronouncement was preposterous—a young girl traveling all that distance alone, she couldn't think of such a thing. Even though I was eighteen, Mother always referred to me as a young girl. Eventually she relented. She was anxious for me somehow to go to college so I would have a profession to fall back on. "We can't leave you a lot of money," she often said, "but we want to leave you prepared to take care of yourself and any children you might have. Widows so often have to run boardinghouses."

Now, beside the Greyhound bus, Mother fretted. Fearful dangers lurked in California: earthquakes, infantile paralysis, evil strangers. Heaven only knew what might happen to a young, inexperienced girl. "If she doesn't have any sense now, she never will have," my father said.

"Maybe we should have packed your galoshes," fussed Mother. "It must rain down there sometime."

Because Dad was present, I did not say, "Oh, *Mother*." Instead I said, "I might not need them," and then, to soothe her, "and you can always mail them if I do." I had no intention of wearing galoshes in California, not ever, no matter how much it rained, if it ever did rain. Postcards did not show rain in California, and the only rain in movies seemed to be raging storms at sea with sails ripping, masts broken, and sailors washed overboard.

What I really wanted at that moment was to tell my father how grateful I was to him for insisting I should leave, but I could not, not in front of Mother, who worked so hard, who made such sacrifices for me. The Greyhound driver, jaunty in his uniform, bounded out of the station and onto the bus. "Well, I guess I'd better get on," I said. Beneath my hidden elation I was nervous about such a long journey even though Mother had written to former neighbors and arranged for them to meet me and put me up overnight in San Francisco and in Los Angeles.

Dad kissed me. Mother said, "Be a good girl and don't forget to write."

"I won't," I promised. None of us noticed that Mother's requests required two different answers, but of course I always had been, mostly, a good girl. A lovely girl, people said, pleasing Mother and annoying me, for I did not feel lovely, not one bit. I felt restless, angry, rebellious, disloyal, and guilty.

In the bus, I looked down at my parents, who suddenly seemed older. I felt as if I had aged them. We exchanged waves and weak smiles, the driver started the motor and shifted gears, and the bus lumbered out of the station, heading south and away from, I hoped, the Depression and all the grief it had brought to my family and to Oregon. I was limp from the emotion of departure, but I was free!

As the bus rolled along the two-lane highway, I pressed my face against the window and tried to memorize all the scenes that meant so much to me: the falls at Oregon City, where my great-grandfather had built the first mill in Oregon; the little white church squeezed between two poplars that had grown so large they seemed about to lift the building from its foundations, the church where my best friend, Claudine, planned to be married someday; the water tower at Canby that marked the turnoff for Claudine's family cabin on the Pudding River where I had spent many relaxed summer days. On, on we rode, with farms and woods fading in dusk and smoke.

The bus stopped at Salem, which brought back a memory that made me smile. My parents had once taken me to Salem because Mother felt visiting the state capital was every citizen's duty and because she wanted me to see the State Home for Girls so I would know what happened to girls who "went bad." Although I was a conscientious girl, a good student more interested in the high school paper, the literary club, and sewing than in boys, Mother worried about my "going bad," as if I were an apple.

The state home had seemed to me a beautiful place where the girls' rooms, looking out on lawns and old trees, were neat, practical, and attractive, quite different from my own room, where I slept in my great-grandfather's creaky four-poster bed, which Mother had festooned with a ruffled pink voile bedspread to make it look feminine. She had also draped an old dresser with more pink voile. My wallpaper was a pretty melding of pastel flowers, but the windows looked out on the neighbors' tan Stonetone stucco house. Mother's Salem lesson in morality had been lost on me. A room in the state home had seemed so pleasant and so convenient it was almost worth going bad for, not that I ever expected to have a chance. I was such a lovely girl.

As the bus rolled out of the capital into darkness, elation faded to sadness and then to grief. Mother, Dad, and the Depression. Joy seemed to have drained out of Mother, who would have been happy teaching but whose credential had not been valid for years, and in those days, work went only to men, single women, or married women whose husbands were disabled. Dad had grown quiet after he had given in and sold the farm that had been in the family for three generations. His abundant harvests had not brought fair prices in the 1920s, and farm life was too strenuous for my small, intense mother. Dad was never comfortable with city life and was lucky, in those grim days, to have a job at all, a job managing the safe-deposit vault in the basement of a bank, a job he disliked. Now I was the focus of my parents' hopes; I must be educated no matter what sacrifices had to be made. I longed to have my parents happy, to share, not sacrifice. The burden of guilt was heavy.

Curled up on two seats, I slept lightly, aware that the bus was laboring over the Siskiyou Mountains. As the sun rose, we pulled into an Agricultural Station shed in a place my bus timetable said was Hornbrook. I was actually in California! The driver ordered sleepy, muttering passengers off the bus with their hand luggage, which we were required to open for inspectors looking for wicked Oregon insects that might destroy California's rich crops. Passengers grumbled. Couldn't inspectors see that insects could fly across the border? I helped eat some of the fruit passengers would not allow to be confiscated, including oranges imported from California that were refused re-admittance.

Back on the bus. A greasy breakfast in Weed, a lumber town fragrant with the resinous smell of sawdust. Mount Shasta, a dumpy mountain when compared with beautiful Mount Hood and the perfect cone of Mount St. Helens, Portland's backdrops. The bus rolled on down the mountains to flat, khaki-colored land where something must have grown because every few miles we passed corrugated metal warehouses with DEPEW painted on the roofs. Dirt-colored hills in the distance did not help. The landscape was all so barren and ugly, so different from my postcard dreams, and the worst part was there was *no water in the rivers*. Never in my life had I seen a dry riverbed. At rest stops I felt as if I were wading through the shimmering heat. After a noontime tuna-fish sandwich and glass of milk, I closed my eyes to shut out the barren land of DEPEW. This was not the California I expected. I felt too dejected to attempt conversation with seatmates.

In late afternoon a hint of cool air drifted through open windows. Passengers sat up, tried to smooth clothes and pat hair into place. Where there was a breeze there was hope. We crossed the Sacramento River and were revived by the sight of water, passed through the stench of oil refineries, saw San Francisco Bay. Farther, on the left, brown hills were punctuated by a white tower. "What is that?" I asked the woman who had taken the seat next to me.

"That's the Campanile on the University of California campus," she said. *Campanile.* What a beautiful word. "And over there," she said, pointing to an island in the bay, "is Alcatraz."

Alcatraz! I was actually seeing the notorious prison. Al Capone, gangsters, machine guns, bodies lying in the streets, just like the movies. Wait till I told my friends in Portland I had actually seen Alcatraz. To the left of Alcatraz, San Francisco was silhouetted against the setting sun. I perked up. The land of DEPEW was behind; excitement lay ahead.

The ferry ride across the bay made me feel like a world traveler. Overnight case in hand, I walked off the ferry into the grim, gray ferry building, where—what a relief—I was met by former Portland neighbors, Mr. and Mrs. Reeves and their daughter, Evelyn, two years older than I, who, when we were in grammar school, had rippled through "Rustle of Spring" on the piano while I plunked miserably through "The Happy Farmer." Even though the Reeveses had not seen me for several years, and nearly twenty-four hours on a bus had left me rumpled and unwashed, they welcomed me so warmly and seemed so dear and so familiar that I forgave Evelyn her efficient rippling and rustling on the piano.

San Francisco! Mother had told me of seeing rubble from the 1906 earthquake when she and her two cousins Verna and Lora had come out west to teach school and to seek adventure, but neither her description nor postcards had prepared me for such a city. Buildings taller than any in Portland, stucco houses shoulder to shoulder, up and down hills, sitting on top of their own garages with aprons of lawn so tiny they could be cut with scissors.

The Reeveses drove to their apartment, which had rooms as large as those in a house. In Portland, Mother discouraged me from associating with friends who lived in apartments because, according to Mother, apartment dwellers were not "substantial." Substantial people, by Mother's definition, lived in houses, mowed lawns, pruned roses.

And here in San Francisco, the Reeveses, substantial as all get-out, lived respectably in an apartment furnished with the familiar fringed lamp shades and overstuffed mohair furniture seen in so many Portland houses. Mrs. Reeves served lamb chops for dinner. I had never tasted lamb because Dad, as a boy on the farm, had eaten so much mutton he vowed never to eat any part of a sheep again. The chops were delicious. Dessert, *fresh* figs with cream, soft sweet circles, cream-colored, with pink spoke-like centers, delectable as well as beautiful. In Portland figs were tan, dried, stewed, and "good for what ails you."

During dinner, when Mr. Reeves told me the city hall was trimmed with real gold, I believed him. Conversation bloomed with colorful words: Marina, Presidio, Hetch Hetchy, Embarcadero, commuter. "What's a commuter?" I asked, never having heard the word. Evelyn explained that to commute was to travel regularly back and forth between two places. She commuted from home by streetcar, ferry, and train to the University of California. In Portland people did not commute. They walked a block or two to a bus or streetcar line, or if they had a car and could afford gas, they drove.

The next morning the Reeveses put me on a bus to Los Angeles. Courage intact, I settled myself, prepared to enjoy the rest of my journey. Two drunken sailors who had taken the backseat sang until they fell asleep. As we drove through San Jose, feathery fronds of pepper trees stroked the top of the bus. My seat partner, a man old enough to be my father, wanted to talk. Mother had warned me about talking to strangers, but she had not told me I should not listen, so I listened. The man said he was supposed to be in Nevada for six weeks to establish residence so he could divorce his wife. He had slipped away to find his daughter, who had run off with a gangster. Divorce was almost unheard of in my neighborhood in Portland in the 1930s. As for gangsters, they existed in Chicago, on Alcatraz, but mostly in the movies. I couldn't wait to write to Claudine.

We rolled down the two-lane highway past orchards and acres of lettuce, and, amazing to me, high school boys, unlike Oregon boys, practicing football in shorts. A brief stop in San Luis Obispo, another tuna-fish sandwich, another glass of milk, and, with a nervous eye on the bus, a short walk along a street of white stucco cottages with hedges of lusty red geraniums, real California geraniums growing in the ground in-

14

stead of in pots. Once back on the bus, the man beside me, unburdened of his troubles, fell asleep. Arroyo Grande, Santa Maria, Los Alamos, Spanish place-names that seemed beautiful to me. So many small towns in Oregon were named after early settlers: Barlow, Heppner, Boring. Some were named after settlers' wives: Beulah, Ada. Others reflected pioneer feelings: Sweet Home, Remote, Sublimity. Still others had Indian names: Owyhee, Yoncalla, Umatilla. I had always found Oregon place-names interesting because they revealed so much about the past, but somehow, as I consulted my timetable, I felt they lacked the musical sounds of Los Olivos, Santa Ynez, Goleta along Highway 101. After a rest stop in Santa Barbara, I must have fallen asleep, for my next recollection is of darkness and of the bus pulling into the Los Angeles Greyhound station.

Stiff and rumpled, with my overnight bag in hand, I climbed off the bus and searched for the familiar faces of friends who were to meet me. No one, not Rowena Reed, her mother, or her sister, was in sight. I had not seen them for at least four years, since they had boarded with a widow in the next block in Portland. Could they have changed so much I did not recognize them? Had I changed so much? Had they forgotten me?

Even with five dollars rolled in my stocking, I had very little money. The station teemed with exhausted, shabby travelers who seemed menacing and may have been. I did the only thing I could think of: I carried my overnight case into a telephone booth, shut the door, sat down on the case, and burst into tears. After a comforting snivel, I pulled myself together and tried to decide what to do. I had wanted adventure, hadn't I? Well, here it was, staring me in the eye in a bad neighborhood in a strange city. Wasn't this adventure? Of course it was. I reached for the telephone book, but as I did so, I saw familiar, plump Rowena and her mother sitting at a lunch counter.

Rowena and Mrs. Reed were as relieved to see me as I was to see them. They drove me to a restaurant where we sat in a horseshoe-shaped booth upholstered in fake black leather, which seemed both elegant and sinister after the hamburger restaurants popular with high school students in Portland. In those Depression days, no family I knew ate in real restaurants. Rowena and her mother, saying they had already eaten, ordered for me a daunting platter of crab Louis, and for themselves, coffee. Rowena drinking coffee? Such sophistication! No one our age in Portland drank coffee, at least no one I knew. After fatigue, nerves, and excitement allowed me to make a dent in the expensive crab Louis, Rowena helped out by eating half of it. Then Mrs. Reed dropped us off at a court apartment shared by her daughters: two rooms, bath, and kitchenette, one of ten or twelve similar apartments grouped in a U shape around a strip of grass. Mrs. Reed went off to the children's home where she lived and worked as a matron.

Rowena's older sister, Estelle, said, "Hi, Beverly, you've sure changed."

I answered, "Hello, Estelle," but my eyes were on one of their friends, who was standing in the middle of the room wearing a black lace bra and panties. How terribly—I pulled a word from my reading vocabulary that I had never spoken—risqué. *Black* lace underwear! Gosh!

"Hi there," said the very blond friend as she pulled a low-cut dress over her head. Didn't California girls wear slips, I wondered, or marveled. As she clamped a curler on her eyelashes, she said, "I'm madly in love with a race car driver, so I'm going to the races." On her way out the door she said over her shoulder, "I'm going to have him, and I don't care how I get him."

I was shocked, but Rowena and Estelle did not seem to think there was anything unusual about this scene, so I tried to act nonchalant. *Noncha-*

lant was a favorite word with certain Grant High students who worked to achieve an air of indifference no matter how excited others might be. Now here I was, nonchalant, too.

Rowena said she felt a sore throat coming on. "Some whiskey might help," she said as she took a bottle from a cupboard.

"Real whiskey?" I asked, half expecting her to rub it on the outside of her throat. Prohibition had been repealed the year before, but I had never seen anyone drink so much as a beer.

"Sure," said Rowena. "Want some?"

"No, thanks," I said with my new nonchalance, trying to sound as if I drank whiskey every day but didn't happen to care for it at the moment.

Rowena sipped her whiskey. I watched her and thought with wicked pleasure, If only Mother could see me now!

A New Family, an Old House

The next afternoon, heat baked through the soles of my shoes as I walked into the Ontario Greyhound station, a station as gritty as all the others on my journey. Yes, the stationmaster informed me, my trunk and typewriter had arrived, but the trunk could not leave the station until the agricultural inspector had examined it. He reached for the telephone, the inspector arrived, I unlocked my trunk and watched him paw through my belongings and pronounce them undefiled by Oregon insects and worthy of entry into California.

With shaking hands I found the Clapps' number in the telephone book, a pamphlet compared to Portland's directory, dropped in my nickel, and placed my call. A man answered, Fred Clapp, Verna's husband. "Beverly?" he said. "I'll be right there."

In a few minutes a tall man with curly gray hair strode into the station. He looked like the physical education teacher he was, vigorous, friendly, brisk, and firm. "So you are Beverly," he said in a voice so resonant that, had he raised it, it would have carried the length of a football field.

Fred loaded my trunk and typewriter into an old sedan, a green Rickenbacker, a car I had never heard of. He was not a man for small talk, a relief because I was too reserved to speak freely to a stranger. We drove up Euclid Avenue, Ontario's main street, which appeared to end in mountains. *This* was the California I had imagined. A strip of lawn in the center of Euclid was bordered by a double row of graceful pepper trees. Orange and lemon trees grew in yards along the avenue. Squatty palms grew there, too, but silhouetted against the brilliant blue sky were the tall palms with feather-duster tops pictured in geography books and on postcards.

"We'll stop at Chaffey so you can register,"

Fred said. He was not a man to waste time, money, words, or anything else.

A block and a half from the college, Fred steered the Rickenbacker into a driveway between a row of eucalyptus trees and a gray two-story house that I knew had once been a downtown boardinghouse until Fred bought it for seventy-five dollars, moved it to his property, knocked out partitions, and turned it into a family dwelling. Ahead, in a large garage, I was surprised to see two more Rickenbackers, one a gray sedan and the other a red topless touring car that looked like a big bathtub on wheels.

As Fred hoisted my trunk and typewriter crate out of the car, a German shepherd left his spot in the shade, moseyed over, languidly wagged his tail as if the heat had drained its energy, and returned to flop down in his patch of shade. "His name is Guard" was Fred's introduction.

Verna came out of the house and walked across the lawn with her hand extended. My hand in hers felt comfortable. Her long dark hair, twisted and pinned, made me wish Mother had not bobbed her own beautiful black hair, which I took such pleasure in brushing when I was a little girl. "So you are Beverly," Verna said. "I would have known you anywhere: You look so much like your mother." That's what everyone said.

As Verna led me into the house, I noted that the front door had a bell that twirled and a frosted panel surrounded by squares of crinkled colored glass like the doors of many old houses of my early childhood in Yamhill, Oregon. The living room, converted from two, perhaps three, rooms, was long and narrow, with a high ceiling. I had an impression of a couch and chairs bright with flowered slip-covers, an antique fireplace between bookshelves that reached the ceiling, fresh flowers on a marble-topped table. The side windows looked through eucalyptus trees with peeling bark to an orange grove (a grove, not an orchard!); the front windows looked across the lawn, a privet hedge, and another orange grove to the San Gabriel Mountains.

"I have never seen mountains without trees before," I remarked. In Oregon, mountains that did not have trees were capped with snow.

"Why, they're covered with trees," Verna said, surprised that I could not see trees. The mountains looked brown and desolate to me. In the excitement of my arrival, the significance of my not seeing trees did not occur to either of us.

Verna led me upstairs to my room, explained that it had two doors because it had once been two rooms in the boardinghouse, showed me the bathroom, and left me to freshen up. My room had a slanting ceiling and two sash windows set so low the sills were only a few inches from the floor. Between the windows was a black drop-front desk with a pair of gilded flatirons for bookends, a floor lamp, and an antique chair. The bedspread was Indian cotton with a paisley design softened by many washings. A pair of Japanese prints hung above the bed. At the opposite side of the room was an oak dresser set between two small closets, one with shelves and the other with hangers. Fred had already set my trunk against one of the doors, and my typewriter crate waited for the lid to be unscrewed. The room was as convenient as a room in the Oregon State Home for Girls but much brighter and more attractive.

When Verna left, I went to the window. There was the Chaffey tower, seen through a tangle of strange shrubs and trees, and close to the house—it couldn't be—yes, it was, an *avocado tree*! Alligator pears, some Oregonians called the fruit Claudine and I sometimes bought and shared, if we could scrape up the money. In Oregon, in the 1930s, money for luxuries was "scraped up." And here in the yard was a tree loaded with fruit that reached to the second story. A gray bird with a saucy tail sat in its branches singing an elaborate song, repeating phrases over and over as if he were trying to get them right.

As I turned from the window, I noticed for the first time the wallpaper, the same soft mingling of pastel flowers that covered the walls of my room in Portland almost a thousand miles away. Was this pretty paper part of some conspiracy to remind me of the home I so desperately needed to grow away from? Of course not, I told myself. It was just a coincidence, and coincidences were not unusual in life even though I understood they were best avoided in stories that I planned to write. Someday.

I unlocked my trunk, shook out a cotton dress, and went of to the bathroom, which had once been a boardinghouse bedroom, to take a cool bath and wash away the perspiration that seemed to exude from every pore. A breeze fanned out the yellow curtains. Towel racks labeled with family names printed on adhesive tape lined the walls. Every towel had the name of a different school woven into a stripe: Santa Ana High School, San Bernardino, Riverside, all apparently left behind in the Chaffey High School gym by visiting teams. I dried myself on a Citrus High School towel.

Back in my room, not knowing what to do next, I sat down on the bed, actually *sat* on the bed because there was no one to tell me not to. And then I heard footsteps on the stairs, whispers, and a knock on the door. When I opened it, I faced my cousins Atlee and Virginia.

"We've come to meet you." Virginia, thirteen years old, was small, blond, pert, with a look of spirit and mischief.

"Come on down to supper," Atlee said. He was fifteen, tall, tanned, curly-haired, and handsome.

I followed my cousins downstairs, through another long narrow room, with a rolltop desk in one corner and french doors leading out to the yard, past a dining room table painted gray with red trim, through the kitchen to a screened porch where a table was laid with place mats, the first I had ever seen. Everyone I knew in Portland used tablecloths, washed on Monday, ironed on Tuesday. Mother Clapp, Fred's mother, was introduced. A tall thin woman who wore round spectacles and a cotton dress that reached her ankles, she reminded me of faded photographs of ancestors that we had stored in a trunk at home. A gray cat rubbed against my legs. "A good mouser," someone said, introducing the cat. I was charmed. A house with mice sounded like a story by Beatrix Potter.

My place at the table faced the grove of tidy orange trees that never shed their leaves and the eucalyptus trees with peeling bark that gave off a pleasant, faintly medicinal fragrance in the heat. Verna asked about my parents. Atlee and Virginia were interested in my long bus trip. I described my amazement at waterless rivers and was surprised that no one found dry riverbeds unusual. The whole family was pleasant, relaxed; no one was nervous, tense, or worried. No one mentioned anyone who had lost his job, the high cost of fuel, shoes that needed resoling, or any other Depression subject. The knot of tension between my shoulders slowly loosened. Maybe I really had left the Depression behind.

I began to ask questions. "What are those square gray things I have seen in so many backyards?" Incinerators for burning trash. At home what little trash we had went into the garbage can, the furnace, or the fireplace. "What was the gray bird with the tail that sticks up?" A mockingbird, something I had never expected to see. "Listen to the Mockingbird" was a sad song about a bird singing over a grave that I had struggled to play on the piano when I was in the fifth grade because it was my grandfather's favorite song. Grandpa was pleased and said I played it like a jig.

When we had finished supper, darkness fell as quickly as a curtain, a surprise to someone used to long summer dusks in Oregon. Then I realized I was closer to the equator, and night was falling just as my grammar school geography teacher had described.

Virginia went into the living room to practice her violin, skillfully bowing from "Humoresque" into a piece I recognized, something about "You can do the cha-cha-cha." Atlee found a screwdriver and accompanied me to my room to unscrew the lid of the crate and lift out my typewriter, an old standard model with an unusually long carriage for typing bank documents that Dad bought for a few dollars when a bank he worked for merged with another bank. He bought it because a writer would need a typewriter.

When Atlee left, I unpacked my meager wardrobe: two woolen dresses, one brown serge and the other navy blue, the fabric cut from bolts of cloth that had lain for years on shelves in my grandfather's general merchandise store. "Such beautiful fabric, and nobody appreciates it these days," Mother said. "It will wear forever." I was afraid it would. A skirt made from a remnant, another that I had made from a pair of my father's old gray pants. I had cut them off at the pockets, ripped the seams, washed and turned the fabric, which was perfectly good on the wrong side, and made myself a four-gored skirt to wear with a pink sweater I had knitted. A couple of cotton dresses; a bathing suit; a badly made skirt and jacket left over from high school; my precious bias-cut cream-colored satin formal, which made me feel as if I were slinking around like Jean Harlow in the movies; my white georgette high school graduation dress; a quilted taffeta evening cape, narrow in the shoulders because I had to skimp when I made it from a remnant.

When I finished unpacking, Fred called out, "Come on, Beverly, let's go over to the plunge for a swim." (Plunge, not a swimming pool!) With Atlee and Virginia, we went to the high school plunge, where Fred was the swimming coach. My cousins, who probably learned to swim before they could walk, swam like fish. Having barely passed the Polliwog level at the Camp Fire Girls' camp where we swam in the icy Sandy River, I was embarrassed to swim in front of a coach, but he tactfully did not try to improve my strokes.

Afterward I sat down at the black desk to write a letter home, a bland but reassuring letter my parents would like to receive. I did not mention gangsters, black lace underwear, or whiskey, and somehow I could not tell my hard-pressed parents how released I felt to be in this pleasant old house where meals were eaten on place mats, the cat caught mice, and the family went swimming at night. When I licked and stamped the envelope, I took it downstairs to a table where I had seen outgoing mail waiting.

In the living room Fred and Virginia were sitting on the couch. Fred was reading Shakespeare to his daughter, who leaned her head against his shoulder. I listened a moment before I tiptoed up the stairs to my room, put on my pajamas, turned off the lamp, and stood at the window, looking out into the darkness, now soft as warm velvet with stars nearer and brighter than any I had ever known. I thought of my weary, discouraged father who disliked his job and longed for outdoor life. I thought of my restless, nervous, worried mother, whose sense of fun had been drained by the Depression and who now made me the center of her life to the point where I felt responsible for her happiness. I knew they were thinking of me and missing me more than I, on the brink of a new life, was missing them.

I stood in the dark by the window a long time before I climbed into bed and fell asleep, exhausted.

"Chaffey, Where the Fronded Palm . . ."

My first day of college I wore a pink dress because everyone said pink was my most becoming color. My stomach quivered with nerves: Would anyone speak to me? Would my dress be right? Would college work be difficult? I walked past orange groves to Chaffey Junior College, where I knew no one and no one knew me. The two-story building was new, earthquake-proof, and built in a "modified Spanish style" around a patio with a lawn and shrub-like palms. Oregonians in the 1930s did not have patios, so *patio* as a spoken word was new to me. In reading I had mentally pronounced it "paysho."

The students looked strange to me, for deep tans were the fashion, the darker the more fashionable. I listened to girls compare and admire their tans and talk about how hard they had worked to get them. The tree-shaded streets and a rainy summer in Portland left me feeling ghostly in the midst of so much toasted skin. There seemed to be no particular fashion in clothing as there had been at Grant High. Everyone seemed comfortable, casual, and, best of all, friendly to a new girl.

California girls, I soon discovered from bits of overheard conversation, knew more about sex than the girls I had known in high school. Some had actually done "it." Mothers at home, as far as I knew, did not mention sex to their daughters, apparently thinking that if they kept it secret, sex would go away and their daughters would remain "lovely girls." What little knowledge I possessed, mostly inaccurate, came from Claudine by way of her cousin who went to Jefferson High, where life was apparently faster than at Grant. As I pondered the difference between Portland and California girls, I concluded that what I had read really was right. Women did mature more quickly in the tropics, and any place that grew palm trees had to count as the tropics.

Students, I soon observed, were of four sorts:

those who lived at home in Ontario or in one of the nearby small towns because it was less expensive than going to the university, those who had completed their freshman and sophomore years but were taking extra courses while they tried to save money to go on to the university, those who were going to school because they didn't know what else to do, and those from out of state, like myself, who were living with friends or relatives and taking advantage of tuition-free education. Today, when we pay our state income tax, I recall with gratitude California's generosity during the Depression. Mother often said, "Oregon does nothing to help its young people," and in the 1930s she was right.

Although I had been apprehensive, I soon discovered classes were no more difficult, and sometimes less demanding, than my classes at Grant. Chaffey, it seemed to me, was like a small, friendly high school with older students.

In French, my first class, a good-looking young man with blue eyes and a tan light enough to show he hadn't worked at it sat beside me. Completely at ease, he smiled, said his name was Paul, and asked where I was from. I could scarcely believe it. At Grant, on the first day of school, either boys were too shy to speak to new girls, or they stood in groups looking girls up and down as if they planned to buy them at auction.

In French we were assigned a novel, *Pêcheur d'Islande,* by Pierre Loti, but a more interesting assignment was dividing into pairs to write a dialogue in French that was to be performed in front of the class. I am sure I blushed with pleasure when Paul asked me to be his partner. Because he was studying journalism and working on the school paper, we had trouble finding time to work together, so, with Verna's permission, I invited him to come to the house one evening.

Paul arrived in his old Model T coupe for an evening of serious French composition. When he stepped into the living room, the family tactfully disappeared, leaving Guard snoozing in front of the couch while we went to work at the large library table. What could we write about? And in French? We settled on a dialogue between two strangers on a bus from Oregon to California. We composed a line for Paul to speak that we found hilarious and were to quote that year whenever it rained: "Oregon, bah! *La pluie, la pluie, la pluie!*" We would struggle through a sentence, and our conversation would veer off to some more engrossing subject, ourselves, mostly. Paul said he had noticed me on the first day of school because I was so pink and white in the midst of all those summer tans. I learned that he was four years older than I, drove a school bus, had been delayed in school because he had broken his back in an accident. Now he was worried about his work on the school paper. I tried to comfort him with experience gained on *The Grantonian* my junior year in high school. He seemed grateful for my superior knowledge.

About eleven o'clock Guard woke up, scratched, and rattled his license tags. Fred called down the stairs in his P.E. teacher voice, "You can put him out now, Beverly." For a dreadful instant Paul and I, engrossed in each other, thought Fred was referring to Paul. (Perhaps he was.) When we realized, or assumed, it was time to let the dog out, we laughed. I opened the door for Guard, and Paul left soon after. Happy, I gathered up the feeble skeleton of our dialogue. A young man with interests similar to mine who could laugh, and whose company I enjoyed, actually liked me. I could scarcely believe it after humorless Gerhart in Portland.

First-semester French taught me that male companionship could be pleasant, even fun, a lesson as valuable as any vocabulary memorized for reading knowledge. Despite our French dialogue, in the 1930s most French teachers did not expect us to actually speak the language of a country so far away we could never afford to go there.

This French teacher did an amazing thing: She left to marry a man who ran a Mexican restaurant in a San Francisco hotel. She was replaced by Dr. L. Gardner Miller, a blond young man fresh from France with an authentic French wife, sandals on his feet, and a degree of Docteur de l'Université. That Dr. Miller expected us to actually *speak* French every minute in class came as a shock. He said we did not know enough, and he was right.

The second classroom I entered that first day was History of Drama, an English course taught by Mrs. Ruth Tremaine Kegley. And there was Paul. This time I sat beside him. Mrs. Kegley stood with her left hand on her hip, her right arm extended with her hand palm up, as she spoke of "the cheap, the blatant, the tawdry" plays on Broadway. She savored the shape of the words, as if she expected them to roll out of her mouth, down her arm, and onto the palm of her hand.

History of Drama did leave me with one valuable thought. One of the playwrights—was it Lope de Vega?—believed that ideas were somehow spewed into the atmosphere to be seized by anyone with a receptive mind, and that upon receiving an idea, one should use it immediately because others were sure to pluck the same idea from the spheres. This one wisp of philosophy, no more than a sentence or two from a college course, has haunted me all my writing life.

The required course in hygiene was taught by short, stout Mrs. Harriet Fleming, whose gray hair was twisted and coiled into a snail on top of her head. Mrs. Fleming required us to write a tiresome paper entitled "Health Heroes" and to outline a boring pamphlet on prenatal care. She not only waded through our papers but was the guardian of our morals who chaperoned college dances. She stopped music if she felt it was too fast or too slow. She once attended a dance in a wheelchair with her leg in a cast, a disability that did not stop her from whizzing out onto the dance floor to reprimand a couple she felt were dancing too close to each other. At one dance I attended, she ordered a girl who was wearing a black dress that left one shoulder bare to leave the floor until she covered her shoulder with a sweater or jacket.

Mrs. Fleming did not object to boys lying on the grass on sunny days, but girls must always sit up or they could expect a reprimand. In her class she once informed us that any girl who wore red was "asking for anything she got." Of course word spread throughout Chaffey. The next day every girl who owned a red dress, skirt, or blouse wore it to school.

One day toward the end of the semester, Mrs. Fleming faced the class and said, "Is there anything you would like to ask me? Anything at all?" Silence. We all knew that *anything* was her code word for sex. Experienced girls looked superior and as contemptuous as they dared, several timid girls looked anxious but were afraid of being laughed at, but most of us exchanged looks of amusement. Even though we might have been eager for information, we certainly were not going to risk asking for it in class.

The silence grew embarrassing. Mrs. Fleming repeated, *"Anything at all."* More silence, broken at last by an earnest, colorless girl who raised her hand and asked, "How do you get rid of dandruff?" Mrs. Fleming, visibly let down, gave suggestions while the rest of us stifled our laughter. As the bell rang, I wondered what went on in men's hygiene.

In physical education I was unexpectedly lucky, for the physical therapist decided my metatarsal arches were in need of strengthening. This put me in a remedial class where I picked up marbles with my toes while strong-arched girls ran around in the hot sun chasing a ball with hockey sticks. I was deeply grateful to my metatarsal arches for not measuring up to Chaffey's standards and for sparing me the sweaty misery of chasing a ball with a stick under the hot sun.

When I entered the geology classroom that first day, there was Paul once more. I was taking the class for two reasons: to fulfill a requirement for laboratory science in case I should ever get to a university, and as a small rebellion against Mother, who had remarked when Verna wrote she was studying geology, "What earthly use is geology to Verna?" She did not stop to think that all knowledge is valuable to a librarian.

The class was taught by Mr. Russell Dysart, a man with a wry sense of humor. Once, when we came to take an examination, we saw, at the edge of a map pulled down over the blackboard, the ends of questions, clues to what we should be prepared to answer. We riffled pages of our textbooks hunting for answers to questions we were about to be asked, but when Mr. Dysart raised the map, the blackboard was blank. With an I-fooled-you grin he passed out to his groaning students sections of U.S. Geodetic Survey maps and told us to write down every geological formation we could find. This was the only examination I have ever enjoyed taking. Today, as I fly across the country, I look for mountains, valleys, extinct volcanoes, meadows, oxbow lakes. . . .

The laboratory periods I found tiresome. We studied and identified various rocks. Several times we went on field trips, with Paul driving the bus, and once we looked at the San Andreas Fault. That famous crack in the earth, which I had read about in newspapers, could cause the surface of the earth to quiver, or it could flatten cities, and was a good reason, according to some of my Oregon relatives, for me to steer clear of California, where a building might fall on me or a crack in the earth open and swallow me. Even though the city of Long Beach had recently been reduced to rubble, Californians seemed interested but unworried about the perils of the San Andreas Fault, but then, many Oregonians suspected Californians of being a carefree, irresponsible lot.

Mr. Dysart's class taught me that nothing on earth is stable. Mountains rise only to be worn down. Rivers change courses. Lakes appear; lakes evaporate. Fertile lands become desert. I left the geology classroom realizing that not only was the earth unstable, life, too, was constantly changing.

And then, toward the end of the year, word filtered down from former Chaffey students that the University of California did not accept geology as a laboratory science. My first thought was, All that for nothing. My second thought was that geology was one of the most enlightening courses I had ever taken.

English was my favorite subject, and Mr. Frank Palmer soon became my favorite teacher. He was a tiny man with a wen on the tip of one ear that gave him an elfin look. He sat on a high stool, with his Phi Beta Kappa key attached to the fob chain of his watch, twinkling against his vest. In the 1930s in the heat of Ontario, male teachers wore suits, although not always vests, to class, but of course not all of them had Phi Beta Kappa keys to twinkle.

Mr. Palmer guided us through *Beowulf* and *Macbeth,* which I had studied in high school, *The Mayor of Casterbridge,* biography, essays, and modern American poetry. He required us to learn to spell Nietzsche, the name of a German philosopher I have never had occasion to use. Best of all, he assigned original compositions but instructed us never to use the expression "broaden our horizons" because, he said, "the horizon is the point at which the earth and sky meet, and it is impossible to broaden a point." I never have, even though I am not sure I agree.

Mr. Palmer read many of our compositions

aloud, always in a monotonous voice. No "reading with expression" for Mr. Palmer. His comments were matter-of-fact, and so sparing of praise that we could be sure any compliment was well earned. One of my compositions was a description of a place on the Oregon coast, probably called Devil's Slide, where strollers along the beach were sometimes trapped against a shale cliff by the incoming tide. Anyone trying to climb the disintegrating cliff found himself sliding back toward the hungry breakers. The harder the victim struggled, the more he slid, sometimes fatally.

I wrote an imaginary description of a girl caught on the cliff by a high tide. I recall one sentence from this piece of writing: "Hot tears ran down her cold cheeks." Mr. Palmer paused in his expressionless reading, thought a moment, and said, "That ought to warm them up." The class laughed.

Wresting an A out of Mr. Palmer was a real challenge. A parsimonious, hairsplitting grader, he sometimes wrote B++ or A-- on my papers. For one assignment, the writing of our autobiographies, I found I recalled so much that I described, with fictitious touches, the early years of my life on the family farm in Yamhill, Oregon. For this I was actually awarded an unadorned, unqualified A. I was ecstatic until I turned to the last page and found Mr. Palmer had encircled with his red pencil every *little,* which I had repeated several times, and joined them with a line, like beads on a string. At the bottom of the page was a single word writ large: *TRANSITIONS!* My joy at wresting an A out of Mr. Palmer was not dimmed, but ever after, I tried to be more careful about transitions.

Fun and Family

"I am so happy," I wrote in my diary and to Claudine. In my letters home I did not mention happiness. Of course, my parents did not want me to be unhappy, but I knew that Mother would prefer that I miss her and be, at least a little, homesick. She would not understand my relief at being able to come home from school without her questioning me about my day's activities, mulling them over, and later pointing out how I could improve my behavior.

When I came home from school in Ontario, I eagerly opened the mailbox. Claudine wrote from her dormitory, Jessica Todd Hall, which she referred to as Jessica Todd Hell, at Oregon State Teachers College in Monmouth, where she was a member of the last class to earn a teaching credential in two years. She played the piano for dances so the school wouldn't have to pay an orchestra. Her letters were cheerful, but Claudine was always cheerful.

Another Portland friend, named Virginia, as was my cousin, was, like me, an only child of a possessive mother. This friend wrote of life in a University of Oregon sorority house, where girls who became engaged had to eat their pie without using silverware on the day they made the announcement. The girls held meetings to point out one another's faults. This Virginia's only fault was wearing face powder that was too light, but hard feelings festered among her sorority sisters. I was glad to be at Chaffey. Other friends, unable to continue their educations during the Depression, wrote briefer letters.

The biggest surprise was Mother's letters. She wrote of my friends, and sprightly, humorous accounts of goings-on in our Portland neighborhood. Mother had often said she would like to write, and her letters showed she had talent. I looked forward to her amusing letters, which she obviously enjoyed writing.

Gerhart wrote, too, with no encouragement from me. Part of my joy in life was the distance between us. Once when I stood in the Clapps' front hall looking with distaste at an envelope from Gerhart, Fred told me I could have the post office return it unopened. I considered the consequences. A returned letter would be reported to Mother, who would write that Gerhart was lonely, that I must be nice to him. I gave in, read his boring letter, and answered in a few noncommittal sentences that I hoped would discourage him and satisfy Mother.

Once Mother wrote that Gerhart had driven the nine hundred miles to Ontario to see me, but when he reached the house, decided in an unusual moment of perception that I would not want to see him. He drove back to Portland. Mother was pleased and amused by this episode, which she considered flattering to me, but I was annoyed and refused to be made to feel responsible for Gerhart's happiness. I was free of him at last.

The Depression seemed to have evaporated in the hot sun of Southern California. No one worried about the cost of heating because houses so rarely needed heating. My two woolen dresses were pulled from the closet only two or three times that winter. Food was less expensive than in Oregon and more varied. Fred sometimes brought from Indio a flat of deglet-noor dates, fresh, moist, and mealy, unlike the dried dates I was used to. A fruit new to me, persimmons, which Atlee swiped from a tree down the street, were sweet and so slithery we leaned over the sink to slurp them. The avocado tree beneath my window was bountiful. When we needed oranges, Atlee drove his red Rickenbacker into the grove his family owned with another Chaffey family. Virginia and I pulled oranges from trees until we filled the backseat. Sitting in the old car, I felt lap-deep in fragrant, golden luxury, oranges crisp and more flavorful than any I had ever eaten.

There was, however, one indication of the Depression in Ontario. Wives of men on the Chaffey faculty who also taught were allowed to work only half-time. Verna, the librarian of both the high school and the junior college, worked more than half a day for half pay, especially now that a new earthquake-proof library was under construction. I knew she felt this was unfair, but she enjoyed her work and did not complain. Often, in the evening, I would see her looking through the encyclopedia and other reference books, searching, searching, searching. Librarians, I was to learn, are always haunted by unanswered reference questions.

Verna maintained a remarkable calm toward her children. Once, when we walked home from school together, we found Atlee, Virginia, and two of their friends battling with decayed oranges fallen from the trees across the driveway. The side of the house was thick with rotten oranges. Verna laughed and said, "All right. Now get the hose and wash it off."

Another time, when Verna learned that Atlee had hopped rides on freight trains, she did not reprimand him. Instead she picked up the newspaper and pretended to read. "Why, here's a dreadful story about a boy who tried to hop a freight train, fell under the wheels, and was beheaded." I wondered if Atlee caught on.

Fred understood boys. Atlee had a large room over the garage connected to the bathroom with a door about three feet high. His room was a jumble of tools, comic books, and other boyish clutter that no one told him to clean up, at least as far as I knew. When people criticized Fred for letting Atlee drive around town in his red Rickenbacker, Fred answered, "What do you expect a fifteen-year-old boy to do—hang around Gemmell's drugstore?" He found a broken-down motorcycle for Atlee to tinker with. Atlee worked hard on his motorcycle, and one day, with pops and bangs, got it to run. We all rushed outside to see the miracle: Atlee riding around and around the house on his red motorcycle. He lent me a pair of pants and took me for a wild ride—

at least, it seemed wild—down Euclid Avenue. Everyone who saw us cheered.

Fred, brimming with vigor, was always busy with one project or another. While I lived there, he built a fireplace for barbecuing near the pergola beneath my bedroom windows. He also moved a two-room cottage from Upland, the town that separated Ontario from the mountains, and set it on his property for rental income.

Another time Fred brought home five gallons of cleaning solvent, cleaned the family's clothes, and asked if I had anything that needed cleaning. I did, the navy blue dress with the white collar I had traveled in. The next time I wore the dress, it exuded solvent fumes as my body heat warmed it. I am sure Paul was amused, but he did not comment.

Most amazing of all, to me, was Fred's help with housework. Except for my father's polishing floors, I had never known a man to touch housework. Every morning Fred made a broilerful of crisp toast. Once a week he charged into the laundry room, which was built onto the rear of the house. He churned several loads of laundry through the washing machine and, with the help of anyone who happened to be around, hung them, sometimes by moonlight, on lines in the backyard. Ironing was a social event, or so it seemed to me, with Verna ironing shirts while Atlee, Virginia, and I lined up in front of an ancient commercial-sized mangle, which was heated by gas. "Now!" Fred would order. The three of us fed napkins, sheets, and towels into the contraption while Fred pulled a lever that lowered the top and pressed the linens as they rolled through.

Then one day Fred came home driving a fourth Rickenbacker, which he had bought for twenty-five dollars from a man who heard he was collecting Rickenbackers. Fred laughed about this, and so did the rest of the family. Fred had bought it for spare parts. These automobiles were becoming extinct.

My part in family duties, as outlined by Verna before I came to California, was keeping my room clean and baking two cakes a week. I had brought with me a file of Mother's cake recipes— Oregonians in those days were great cake bakers because cake was a Depression luxury that usually could be assembled from whatever was in the cupboard. I am ashamed to say I did not always bake the two cakes a week expected of me, but I am sure I baked at least one and usually filled in with brownies or apple crisp.

One day Verna brought home an electric mixer, which I found fascinating when the batter rose higher and higher as the beaters spun. *This* was going to be the lightest, fluffiest cake I had ever baked, a cake that would dazzle the family with my skill. Unfortunately, when I removed the cake from the oven, it exhaled all the air I had beaten into it and sank into a flat, dry slab. I tried, not very successfully, to lubricate it with butter-and-powdered-sugar frosting. The family was game and ate it anyway. As Mother said, Verna always did have a sweet tooth.

That cake was not the only kitchen failure that year. Virginia's home economics teacher required girls to cook at home recipes they had studied in class and to bring a note from a parent telling of the result. One afternoon Virginia baked a fragrant chocolate cake, but when she took it from the oven, it looked more like fudge than cake. Together we studied the recipe and discovered that Virginia had forgotten to include flour. She was as crestfallen as her cake.

"Never mind," said Fred. "We'll eat it like candy." Unfortunately, Virginia's cake did not taste like fudge; it tasted like Crisco. Only Fred managed to eat a piece in an attempt to cheer his daughter.

Mother Clapp, who spent most of the day sitting in a low rocker in her room reading her Bible, crept downstairs late afternoons to start dinner. I often joined her to make salad and to set the table. Mother Clapp was such a quiet woman we found little to say to each other, but I felt she was friendly toward me. I enjoyed sharing peaceful moments with her as I laid out the red-and-white place mats and set the table with Blue Willow dishes.

Dinner conversation was cheerful, centering on the events at the high school and junior college. One day Verna brought home an example of her day's work, a can of soy loaf given her by a man who was using the school library to research soybeans, which he felt had undiscovered possibilities. Material for automobile tires, for example. The can was opened, the soybean loaf was heated. We bravely prepared to eat the whole thing because Fred did not approve of waste. Then Atlee threw down his fork and said, "Why don't you say it? It's just like dog food." He was so right we couldn't help laughing, and Guard finished the loaf for us.

Laughter at the dinner table was a new experience for me. My parents often smiled, but laugh out loud, never. The Depression had left us with little to laugh about. And then one day a letter arrived from home. Verna, Mother told me, had written that it was so discouraging to come home from the library to a house with carpets that needed vacuuming and bouquets of dead flowers gathering dust in the living room. Mother said I must run the vacuum cleaner and empty out wilted flowers. I was willing to do this, but why, I wondered, did Verna involve Mother? I loved Verna and was hurt, but after that, when I vacuumed my room, I vacuumed the living room as well. Verna acted as if this were not unusual, and I was too busy being happy to brood about my shortcomings. I had Paul to think about.

When the first issue of the school paper came out, there on the front page was the editor's picture. Paul. He had not said a word to me about being editor when I had so generously shared with him the wisdom gained from my high school journalism. He was amused by my embarrassment; I told him he did not play fair. We both laughed, and Paul chugged down Princeton Street in his Model T coupe to take me to movies in Pomona, to school dances, and out for something to eat afterward. To me he seemed sophisticated because he drank coffee; to him I was amusing because I ordered milk. Afterward he parked in front of the Clapps' privet hedge, where we enjoyed what I referred to in my diary as "long rambling conversations" about school, our lives, our hopes. We both wanted to write.

One evening Paul told me that other men were asking how far our relationship had gone. I was too shocked to do anything but gasp. Paul smiled, rumpled my hair, and said, "I think I know what you like."

What I liked, and for the first time in my life was enjoying, was the companionship of a humorous, congenial young man. After sulky Gerhart and the serious high school boys and Reed College freshmen who trampled my feet at dances, or I trampled theirs, and never seemed particularly congenial, the company of Paul was a joy, and he was understanding of my girlish innocence and enthusiasm. With Paul I did not have to pretend I was having a good time. I really was having a good time. Paul was restoring my faith in young men by helping me to see that a man could be a companion. All I wanted was his company, lots of it.

Sharing a sense of humor was a new experience for me. Paul and I both thought the words of the school song were funny, a song that began, "Chaffey, where the fronded palm uplifted to the sky . . ." The tree we sang about was a scruffy fan palm in front of the building. It had a few green fronds rising above generations of withered fronds drooping against the trunk below.

Although I doubted if Paul really enjoyed dancing, he took me to all the school dances, which I found much more fun than the few dances I had

attended at Grant High, where girls were possessive of boys, couples rarely traded dances, sometimes not at all, and persuading myself I had
enjoyed the evening had scarcely been worth the
effort of cleaning black shoe polish off my white
pumps the next morning.

At Chaffey we had dance programs, which I
had heard Mother tell about but which I thought
had gone out of fashion along with hatpins, corset
covers, hair receivers, and other artifacts of
Mother's youth. We circulated, talked to other
couples, agreed which dances to trade, and
marked them on our programs with tiny pencils
attached with silk cords. Then we danced away
to "Red Sails in the Sunset" and "A Little Bit
Independent," "Blue Moon," and other popular
tunes of the 1930s. Paul and I always sat out
"Tiger Rag" because it was too fast, and at the
end of the evening, when the band played "Good-
night, Sweetheart," Paul held me close.

Sometimes, after the dance, if it was a moonlit
night, we went for a short drive eastward toward
the desert, where ghostly spheres of tumbleweed
rolled across the road. Real tumbleweed, something I had never expected to see, but there it
was, rolling along, the tumbling tumbleweed, just
as in the words of the song.

Even the weather took on a new excitement.

When rain finally came, it fell harder and faster than the gentle rain of Oregon. One evening after a YWCA dinner at school, I found I could not cross Euclid Avenue's deep gutters, now overflowing with water carrying rocks and gravel, swifter than a mountain stream, racing straight from the mountains without curves to slow it down. The town had not had time to set out little bridges at intersections. What to do? I returned to school and telephoned the Clapps. Atlee was dispatched to rescue me and arrived in his Rickenbacker, which he maneuvered close enough so that I could, with the help of his outstretched hand, leap onto the running board and, soaked to the skin, fall into the front seat. My galoshes were still dry in my closet in Portland, my shoes were soggy, and I did not care.

And then the earthquake. One evening when I was studying, the old house began to quiver and then to shake and creak. My floor lamp swayed until I grabbed it. No one had told me what to do in an earthquake, so I sat tight, clutching my lamp, for the few seconds the earth took to calm itself.

"Beverly, did you feel that?" Fred called out. I had indeed. Who could study after such an exciting experience? Books shoved aside, I wrote letters to my parents and to Claudine saying I had just survived an earthquake, a *real* earthquake, just like those we read about in the newspapers. Some years later, earthquakes began to shake up Oregonians, too, but in the 1930s Oregon was considered rock-solid. Only California shook.

Earthquakes were not the only excitement provided by nature. As what passed for winter came to Southern California, Fred turned on the radio every evening at seven o'clock to listen to the frost warnings because he had an orange grove to protect. I had not understood the consequences of these warnings until late one afternoon when I looked out my bedroom window and saw over toward Pomona billows of black smoke. Alarmed, I ran downstairs to tell Verna, "There's a big fire over by Pomona!"

Verna assured me it was not a fire, that the temperature must have suddenly dropped to the point at which smudge pots had to be lit in that area so oily smoke would warm the groves and prevent the oranges from freezing. Those smudge pots affected our social life, I was soon to discover. One night at a school dance, the music stopped and someone announced that the temperature had dropped to the danger point. At this news, a number of young men left the gym to go out into the cold night, leaving their partners to share cars and get home as best they could.

Smudging was dirty for everyone, but it was dangerous for the boys who worked all night to keep the pots filled with oil and who reported to class gray with fatigue and smoke they had not been able to scrub from their pores. Leaping flames casting shadows in the groves were a beautiful sight, hellishly beautiful for the young men who worked through the night and were sometimes badly burned trying to warm themselves by standing too close to the blazing pots in their oil-soaked clothes.

Sometime in the winter, migratory workers from Mexico quietly appeared with ladders and clippers to snip navel oranges from the trees and drop them into canvas bags. Cull oranges, in those days before frozen orange juice, were spread through the groves for fertilizer, and for a few days, until the culls began to decay, Ontario was as fragrant as a vast kettle of marmalade.

And then, in the spring, waxy blossoms burst forth from the orange trees, blossoms with perfume so sweet and so heavy that walking to school seemed dreamy and unreal. Smog had not yet come to Southern California. The skies were blue, and Ontario was an enchanted place.

The enchantment of my new life began to fade when Mother Clapp left to visit a relative, and Verna's mother, my great-aunt Elizabeth, who had been staying with another daughter, came to take her place. Aunt Elizabeth had visited us in Portland, and it was her idea that I spend the winter with the Clapps and go to junior college. I had found her delightful—chatty, vivacious, full of fun, and fashion-conscious in a way I thought unusual for someone her age. I was grateful to her for Verna's invitation and looked forward to seeing my tiny, lively great-aunt again.

To my surprise and discomfort, Aunt Elizabeth began to criticize me, and I began to feel uncomfortable in her company. *She* set the table the way the family liked, she said. I did not understand. Mother Clapp had not complained, and neither had anyone else in the family. She said I took advantage of Verna. On this point, she may have been right, but I did not mean to take advantage. I did the work Verna outlined in her invitation, and after her hint to Mother, did more, but as I look back, I can see that I should have been more helpful.

Aunt Elizabeth also criticized my clothes. Some of my dresses were too tight. Every day after school I had eaten an avocado from the tree beneath my bedroom window, unaware that I was consuming between five and six hundred calories. For the first time in my life I gained weight. Aunt

Elizabeth was right. Some of my clothes were too tight, but I had no money for new clothes.

My biggest clothing problem was my bias-cut Jean Harlow satin formal, which I had waited months to wear to a formal school dance. It now cupped below my bottom and clung in a way that was sure to make Mrs. Fleming banish me from the dance floor. I couldn't bear not to wear it, so I bought an inexpensive two-way stretch girdle to make me thinner. Unfortunately, as Paul and I danced, the girdle began to stretch up and to roll down until it made a thick tire around my waist. Don't let anyone notice, I silently prayed as I stood up straight so I could breathe more easily between trips to the rest room to tug it down.

When Paul took me home and I stepped out onto the running board of his Model T, he unexpectedly put his arms around me, so that I slithered to the ground. He must have felt, and been amused by, the roll around my waist, but he was too kind to let on. I was glad to say good night, run upstairs, and peel off the two-way stretch girdle and take a deep breath once more. I was annoyed because it had stretched up more than out, and I never wore the thing again. Neither did I wear my slinky satin formal.

The last semester of my freshman year was

coming to an end, and I was elected to Alpha Gamma Sigma, the honor society. Late one afternoon, when Verna and I were working in the kitchen, I worked up courage to ask the question that had worried me for some time: "Do you want me to come back next year?" Even though I had been invited only for the winter, I hoped I would be welcome for another year.

Verna paused in whatever she was doing and answered, "Fred and I have been discussing it, and we don't see how we would have room for you because both grandmothers will live with us next year."

"Oh." My disappointment was deep. I thought a moment before I said, "I wonder what I can do next."

Verna was sympathetic. "Can't your grandfather help you?"

Although Grandpa Atlee sent me five dollars every month, I was sure Mother would not let me ask him for more substantial help. Asking without her permission did not occur to me. Many years later, when the time came for me to go through Mother's possessions, I found a bundle of Grandpa's canceled checks. He had paid for the entire college education of his other grandchild, a grandson who became a distinguished electrical engineer.

After my conversation with Verna, I wrote in a scrawl diagonally across the last page of my diary, "What am I going to do now?" With that I ceased keeping a diary and pushed worry about the future to the back of my mind. I wanted to cling to every moment, and one of the most important was the distribution of the *Argus,* the yearbook. Embossed on the cover was an inaccurate picture of Chaffey's tower, the wrong variety of palm tree, a shield with a strange heraldic animal, possibly a griffin (why?), and the words:

Loyalty ♥ ♥ ♥
Achievement and
The Spirit of
Honor ♥ ♥ ♥

Before and after classes, and sometimes in class, students wrote sentimental messages in one another's books: "Don't forget drama class. Loads of luck." "Be good and everything." "Here's wishing a very nice girl a very nice future. It's been swell having you in a lot of my classes."

Exchanging messages with Paul was an event much too important to be hurried at school even though by now I sensed he was growing bored with my girlish enthusiasm. In his Model T we rattled out toward the mountains, traded yearbooks, and began to write. He wrote two pages, beginning: "My dear Beverly: Here I sit under a sweeping oak tree some nine months after I first saw you . . ." and going on to tell me I had helped make his year complete; advising me to have more confidence in myself—"You really have everything it takes, plus a very fine understanding of people"; and cautioning me about trying to read between the lines—"Unfortunately—or fortunately—no one has found the key. . . ." He ended: "I believe you will understand and appreciate what I have tried to say. You have been a wonderful pal, loyal friend and a perfectly swell girl friend. May we meet again my dear and often. With love, Paul."

Key? Key to what? His heart, presumably. Oh dear. Paul, like many others, had misinterpreted my feelings for him and seen as serious love what was really my joy in my new life and in the beauty of the world around me, and my pleasure in sharing common interests with a young man. Best of all, Paul was fun. The misreading of my girlish crush by others had embarrassed me, and now Paul's reference to "the key" embarrassed me even more. I wonder what I wrote in his *Argus*. Something cautious, I am sure.

A few days before I was to leave, Verna turned to me in the kitchen and said, "Beverly, I don't

62

want you ever to tell your mother you didn't make good grades because I made you work too hard." I was stunned, too stunned to speak. Why did she think I would say a thing like that? I had fulfilled the duties outlined before I came and more and would willingly have done anything she asked of me. But she never asked, just wrote a hint to Mother. Finally I managed to say, "But I did make good grades." Didn't she remember that I was a member of the honor society?

That was the end of the matter, but for many years I thought about the incident, which left me with an insecurity. Was I failing to please when I thought I was doing the right thing?

Verna's feelings toward me did not appear to change. She was interested, kind, and helpful as always. I went with her in the gray Rickenbacker to Los Angeles, where she attended a library association's monthly book breakfast. So I wouldn't get lost, Fred had me memorize the streets I must stay on: Main, Spring, Broadway, Hill, Olive, Grand, Hope, Flower, and Figueroa. Once we went to the Orange Belt Emporium in Pomona to choose yarn for a suit she had asked me to knit for her during the summer. She had always wanted a hand-knit suit even though Fred held forth on the foolishness of knitting. It was a waste of time, he said. Machine-knit clothes cost less. Verna and I knew machine-knit clothes could not compare with hand-knit in beauty and texture. Besides, she offered to pay me twenty dollars.

The last day, the day I packed my trunk, Atlee unexpectedly asked me to go downtown for a milk shake. I was both pleased and surprised and have often wondered if the invitation was his own idea. That evening, after my typewriter was screwed into its crate once more, Paul came to bring me a box of candy and to say good-bye and wish me luck in whatever was to happen next in my life. He had a summer job as night watchman at the Little Theater in Padua Hills and in September would go to the University of Southern California on a journalism scholarship. We agreed to write, but in my heart I doubted if I would ever see him again.

The next morning, as I was about to say good-bye to the family on the driveway, Fred looked at my awkward typewriter crate and issued an order: "Atlee, get the brace and bit and some rope from the garage. Let's make Beverly's typewriter easier to handle." Atlee obeyed, and the two quickly unscrewed the lid, bored holes in the crate, knotted rope handles through them, and screwed the lid back on. I was grateful for this last act of kindness, and I am sure it was appreciated by porters and taxi drivers who were stuck with handling the unwieldy wooden box.

Fred and Atlee lifted my trunk and typewriter into the green Rickenbacker, I said good-bye to Verna and Virginia, and Fred drove me to the Greyhound station. As my bus pulled out, I burst into tears. "Why, she's crying," I heard someone say.

Yes, I was crying. I had been so happy and now I faced a blank future. What would happen next? What *could* happen next? I had no idea, but I did know that year had changed my life forever.

Desperation and Inspiration

The long journey in reverse with no overnight stops in California. "We don't want to impose on friends," Mother had written. The land of DEPEW had not changed, but I had. Beauty, to my eyes, now replaced desolation. The silvery gray warehouses made a foreground. As the sun moved across the brilliant sky, hills and barren fields turned to gold, and shadows shifted across canyons. An occasional live oak, lonely and determined, cast its lengthening shadow as it clung to a hill. Would I ever see this golden state again? Probably not. Sadly I concentrated on remembering all that had given me so much happiness in the past year.

As California rolled by, I became aware of the

man seated next to me, who seemed as dejected as I. He glanced at me and initiated a conversation. He told me he was a deadheading Greyhound driver who drove at night but did not know how much longer he could work because he was developing pinpoint eye. Curiosity overcame Mother's warnings about not talking to strangers. What was pinpoint eye? He explained that constantly facing oncoming headlights was affecting the pupils of his eyes, which contracted as the lights approached but no longer expanded as rapidly as they should when the lights passed. He was worried about finding work when he could no longer drive.

I felt as if the Depression were coming closer with every revolution of the Greyhound's wheels. The man talked on about his troubles as the bus carried us into Oregon without stopping for luggage inspection. Oregon trusted California's insects to observe state lines. We pulled into Ashland, where Dad wanted me to spend the night in a bus stop hotel to break up my long trip. Mother had written precise instructions about registering at a hotel along with her usual warnings about strangers. As we climbed off the bus, the deadheading driver asked me if I would have dinner with him. The invitation was so unexpected I did not know how to answer, and so in my confusion I said abruptly, "No, thank you!" The man looked as if I had slapped him. I quickly registered and fled to my room, where, haunted by the look on the man's face, I came to realize he was a decent, lonely man. I went down to the coffee shop hoping to find him and tell him I had not meant to be rude. He was nowhere in sight. I sat down at the counter and ate the usual Greyhound meal of hamburger "steak," canned peas, and mashed potatoes with a crater filled with tasteless brown gravy.

The next afternoon, after an eye-soothing ride up the Willamette Valley, I saw Mother and Dad, smiling but anxious, waiting for my bus. Their relief when I disembarked, rumpled but alive and well, was obvious, and they plied me with questions. Yes, Oregon looked good to me; everything was so green and the snow-capped mountains so beautiful. Yes, the trip was tiring, but the night in Ashland helped. Yes, I had gained weight. Yes, I was glad to be home. The truth of this answer was questionable, but I could not hurt the feelings of my loving parents by saying, "Sort of."

On the streetcar ride home, Mother and I talked and laughed while Dad, quiet as always, chuckled. After supper, friends dropped in to trade anecdotes of our first year away from home, or their first year working. There was much laughter, and Mother served ice cream and cake. She enjoyed my friends and they enjoyed her. After all, she did not expect them to be perfect.

The next day, I washed California out of my hair and was unpacking my trunk when Gerhart came to see me. I was cool, courteous, and, I hoped, discouraging. He did not stay long.

That evening, when Mother and I were in the kitchen washing and drying dishes, she began what I thought of as a cross-examination, just as she had when I had come home after a day in high school.

"Did Paul ask you to marry him?"

"No."

"Why didn't he?"

"Probably because he didn't want to marry me, and besides, he has two more years of college." I did not admit to a passage in my diary in which I had written that Paul once said he could get serious about me. I had passed this off lightly, not really believing he meant it. Still, I wondered. "Anyway, I'm not interested in marrying anyone at this time in my life," I told Mother.

"Well!" said Mother. "If I had seen as much of a young man as you have seen of Paul, I would have had a marriage proposal."

Was I supposed to feel like a failure because I had enjoyed the company of a congenial young man? At this point I lost my calm. "Mother!" I was exasperated. "I am not out to collect scalps!"

Mother's lips tightened. She said nothing; neither did I. I was home, really home.

Years later, when I was clearing out Mother's house, I found a box of eight or ten photographs of young men in the high stiff collars worn in the period of her youth. On the back of each was written a name and the words "An admirer." Mother had treasured her scalps.

That summer I knit my nervous energy and my worries into Verna's suit. I was eager to earn money, difficult for women during the Depression. When I mentioned applying for work at Meier & Frank, a department store that hired young women for summer work, I was told by my parents no daughter of theirs would be seen working there. Some of my friends were going out to pick strawberries, but when I suggested going, Mother said, "Absolutely not," which was just as well. The work was backbreaking. I suggested going out to Banks, staying with my grandparents, and working in the woods with the local women who cut sword ferns to be shipped to florists in New York. Once more, no. Mother often said I must stand on my own two feet, and now she wouldn't let me.

Then there was the problem of my father's vacation. "He does need a change," Mother told me. "He needs to get away from the city."

What could we do? Where could we go? In those Depression days, most people were too proud to admit to being hard up, but they were quietly understanding and offered help to one another. The Klums, Claudine's parents, offered us the use of their cabin on the Pudding River for about ten days. One of my father's customers at the bank who ran a secondhand car lot offered the use of a car. "Nobody's buying cars these days," he told Dad. "You might as well get some use out of it. Otherwise it will just sit there and rust." We loaded the big old sedan with provisions, a tent, two army cots, and bedding and took off for the Pudding River. "Puddin'," Claudine and I called it.

The Klums' one-room cabin was located in a campground under Douglas fir trees on flat land bordered by the river that was part of the Colvin brothers' farm. We carried water in five-gallon cans from one of the farmhouses and used toilets in the communal bathhouse.

Mother, always anxious not to impose, insisted we use the cabin as little as possible. Dad pitched the tent nearby and set up the camp cots. I slept on a couch on the cabin porch with my head on a pillow embroidered with pepper berries and the words "I love you, California." We cooked on an outdoor camp stove under the trees. The borrowed car was parked nearby, awaiting our journey home. Dad felt it should be used strictly for transportation to Puddin' and back to Portland. No joyriding for us.

Dad and I swam. Mother had never learned how. "My head goes down and my feet go up" was her reason, so she sat in the shade with a book. I read, knit, and tried to think of a solution for my future, a problem we had avoided mentioning. Dad hiked, refreshed by the sight of farmland once more.

On the weekend the campground took on new life. A stream of old cars arrived bearing campers and picnickers, a cash crop harvested by the Colvin children, who collected admission fees at the gate. Picnickers parked their cars, marked their spaces on tables with boxes and baskets, built fires in camp stoves, and organized baseball games in the meadow and horseshoe-pitching tournaments under the firs, where chipmunks raced and scolded. Cooling watermelons, penned in by rocks, bobbed in the river under the alders, and smoke drifted through the trees. Children hurried into their bathing suits to swim. High school students, those who had nickels to spare, fed the jukebox. Big-band music—Artie Shaw,

Glenn Miller, Tommy Dorsey, Benny Goodman—mingled with laughter, shouts, cautions to children, the thwack of a bat against a ball, the clang of horseshoes against metal stakes, the thump of the diving board, splashing in the river.

Then came the fragrance of picnics: chicken and hamburgers frying, coffee boiling. Late afternoon, more nickels were dug from deep in pockets, and more music swung out under the firs. Everyone danced: boys with girls, husbands with wives, mothers instructing their young sons, fathers helping small girls eager to learn to dance, women with one another. As dusk crept in and mist rose from the river, picnickers left the dance floor, loaded their cars, and joggled down the rough road past the cabin, and I was alone with my parents once more.

Late one afternoon I was sitting on a picnic table near the river knitting and enjoying silence and solitude while I tried to work out my future. No one had mentioned business school, but I could see no other possibility. Living at home, long carsick streetcar rides, the racket of a roomful of typewriters, unbearable pressure for speed and accuracy, the unknown horrors of shorthand, bookkeeping, another carsick ride home. There had to be a way out. There *had* to be.

My thoughts were interrupted by Dad calling

me. I was startled to face Mother and Dad, both angry. Mother said, "Just because you have gone to college you needn't feel so snooty toward your parents."

Now I was angry. "What's wrong with going off by myself to try to think out what I can do next?" I demanded. "I can't sit around home all my life. What am I supposed to do?"

This outburst surprised and calmed my parents. Finally the three of us could worry together. But I knew I could not waste time worrying, or, as Mother would say, stewing. I had to *do* something and do it soon.

In desperation I found inspiration. At Chaffey I had met a girl from Washington State who had spent the winter with a faculty family in Ontario and who had not been invited back. Her first name was Norma. Norma what? I did not know. I pieced together snippets of memory. She was tall, blond, and athletic and was planning on majoring in physical education. Her home was in the mountains, where her father worked for the Seattle Watershed. Verna had once told me that the woman Norma lived with was annoyed because Norma came home from school, sat down, and read the paper. That was all I knew about her. If I could find out where she received her mail, perhaps I could write and suggest we share an apartment in Ontario for our sophomore year, if Ontario had apartments. I couldn't recall seeing any. I did not mention my idea to Mother and Dad, who might crush it before it was fully hatched.

Then one night, as I lay awake trying to recall more about Norma, rain began to fall, quite hard for summer, and I fell asleep to the sound of heavy drops pounding on the porch roof. Sometime in the night, I was awakened by male voices nearby. I could see the beam of a flashlight and two shadowy figures on bicycles.

"This must be it," I heard one of them say. They dismounted their bicycles and approached the cabin.

"What do you want?" I asked bravely as I sat up, the blanket pulled to my chin.

"Is this where the Bunns are staying?" The voice was that of a high school boy. The pair stepped onto the porch at the foot of my bed, out of the rain.

Dad had heard. I saw him, dimly, by the wavering light of his flashlight as he tried to hold it while he buttoned his pants. Rain had plastered his hair to his forehead. "What's going on here?" he demanded.

"We have a telegram for Mrs. Bunn," one of the sodden boys answered.

A telegram! And in the middle of the night. No one ever sent telegrams or made long-distance calls unless there was a calamity.

"Where did you kids come from?" Dad asked as he signed for the telegram.

"Canby," one answered. "The telegraph office thought we could find you out here."

"Some ride in the rain." Dad reached into his pocket for change to give to the soggy pair. They thanked him, grateful for anything they were given, and rode off into the darkness by the unsteady beam of their flashlight.

But who would send a telegram so important it had to be delivered in the woods in the middle of a rainy night? By now Mother, with a sweater over her nightgown, had joined us. We huddled around the flashlight while she tore open the yellow envelope. "Why, it's from Verna," she said. "Aunt Elizabeth died."

"She was well when I left in June." I didn't know what else to say.

(Today I wonder if her personality change might have been due to a health problem. Perhaps I did not deserve all her nagging. Perhaps I did. I'll never know.)

"I wonder how Western Union tracked us down," said Dad.

"Poor Aunt Elizabeth," said Mother, and we all went back to bed with our own thoughts.

The next morning the sun was shining, Mother was smiling, chipmunks scampered through the trees, and Dad had built a fire in the camp stove. "Now you can go back and stay with Verna and Fred another year," said Mother as she laid bacon in the frying pan.

I was sure I could not. "If they invite me," I said. Now, having thought of an alternative plan, I was not entirely sure I wanted to stay with relatives again. Even though I loved them all, there had been moments of discomfort, of not knowing where I stood, of feeling I was not doing the right thing. Beneath my happiness there had been some strain, even before the arrival of Aunt Elizabeth.

"But Verna promised you two years of college." This was wishful thinking on Mother's part. I tried to remind her that I had been invited to spend the winter. "No," insisted Mother, and Mother was a great insister, firm and unrelenting. "She promised two years."

In a day or two we packed up the car and headed for home, the mailbox, and my yearbook. A welcome letter from Paul was waiting. After I read it, I studied my yearbook for Norma's picture. There she was, N. Crews, a tall girl in the

77

last row of the Women's Athletic Association picture. N. Crews was also on a victorious hockey team and the freshmen women's basketball team. I looked for a written farewell message but found none. Obviously N. Crews and I had little in common, but still . . .

Mother and I wrote letters of condolence to Verna, who responded by saying her mother's death was quite unexpected and that Atlee, now sixteen, had accompanied his grandmother's body by train to their family cemetery in Michigan. She said nothing about my returning.

Mother was indignant. Why hadn't Verna mentioned my coming back? What was wrong that I was no longer welcome?

"Mother, just forget it," I begged. "I had one happy year. Don't spoil it."

But Mother would not forget. She wrote to both Verna and Lora. I did not know what she said and did not want to know. Whatever it was, she received tactful answers but no invitation for me. Mother despaired. Her cousins must not consider me the perfect daughter she had struggled to bring me up to be. What had I done wrong, she insisted on knowing. I wasn't sure, I told her, but I supposed I hadn't done enough housework.

"Housework!" Mother was indignant as well as

desperate. "You weren't invited to do housework. You were invited to bake cake."

"And I did bake cake," I reminded her. I waited for Mother to calm down before I brought up my idea of asking Norma, if I could reach her, to share an apartment. At first Mother was horrified. I would do no such thing. Two girls in an apartment? It would never do.

Once more Dad reminded Mother that if I didn't have any sense by then, I never would have. Gradually she softened and asked the usual motherly questions. Just what sort of girl was this Norma? I described her as a picture of health, full of fun, a model student, a hard worker, a really lovely person. I was sure about the picture of health, and produced my yearbook to prove it, but I was not so sure about the rest of my fanciful description. With such different interests, we had not shared classes.

Mother reluctantly allowed me to write to Norma and offer my suggestion. But how? I must have sent my letter in care of the Seattle Watershed. Somehow it reached her. In a few days I received an enthusiastic answer. She, too, had longed to go back to Chaffey, and her parents agreed to our sharing an apartment. Mother wrote to Verna, who volunteered to look for an apartment.

Letters flew back and forth. My parents could let me have fifteen dollars a month, and my grandfather would continue to send my five. Norma would have about the same amount. I found remnants in a department store basement and made some dresses that weren't too tight, wrote frequently to Paul, watched eagerly for his less frequent letters, knit swiftly around and around Verna's skirt, finished it, started the jacket.

Claudine invited me to spend a few days at Puddin', an invitation I was overjoyed to accept, and I went, knitting all the way. I finished knitting the jacket and started the lace blouse on larger needles. Somehow, by the first of September, that, too, was finished. I had earned twenty dollars! Twenty whole dollars, the most I had ever earned.

Verna wrote that she had found us a two-room, share-a-bath apartment next door to the public library, which made it, in Mother's eyes, respectable. The rent was fifteen dollars a month. Joyfully I packed my trunk, this time including sheets, dish towels, and lavender bath towels with purple monograms (Meier & Frank had had a sale), which cushioned a sandwich toaster Mother had bought for us. I met smiling Norma at the Greyhound depot and brought her home on a streetcar. Mother studied her, relaxed, and took me aside to whisper, "It's going to be all right. She's a nice girl." I was relieved that Mother was relieved.

Late the next afternoon, Norma and I took off on the bus for California. During the uncomfortable night, she confided that until my letter arrived she had been desolate with longing to return to Chaffey when she was not invited back, but because she had two older brothers in college, she had to wait her turn to continue her education until they graduated. Her parents could not afford three children in universities at the same time. They had been as relieved as Norma by my letter, and her mother apparently did not worry about "just what sort of girl is this Beverly."

We had planned to stay two nights at the San Francisco YWCA so we could spend a day sightseeing, but after one night we were so eager to get to Ontario, as if we were afraid it might have disappeared during the summer, that we consulted the bus schedule and found the next bus for Los Angeles left in late afternoon. We arrived at the station early and each rented a pillow, a necessity, not an extravagance, we decided, after our previous night on the bus.

We had not noticed that this bus traveled by Highway 99, a much longer, hotter trip than the route I had taken the year before. It was a miserable journey with many stops.

Bakersfield, in those days before air-conditioning, was an oven at midnight. Inside the station hundreds of sinister-looking large-winged insects swooped and flopped. Norma and I were too sweaty to eat and beat off bugs, so we climbed back onto the bus. Neither of us could sleep. I wondered if this bus driver had pinpoint eye.

Daylight. In Los Angeles we ate a greasy breakfast at a counter in the station before we changed to a bus bound for Ontario, where we arrived grimy and rumpled. After the ritual agricultural inspection of our trunks, we walked, overnight cases in hand, to our new address, a big old gray house on Euclid Avenue.

The landlady, Mrs. Tuckness, who was also a dressmaker, led us upstairs to the two front rooms, identical in size and separated by a closet with a curtain of eucalyptus buds strung like beads. The floors were painted "robin's egg blue" and had large linoleum rugs. Each room had a door into the hall. We were not given keys and did not think this unusual. After we paid our rent, Mrs. Tuckness said, "It is going to be fun to have girls around, and as long as I can hear noise when young men come to call I won't worry about you."

We stepped out onto the shaky balcony outside our living-bedroom to look at the library and the palms, grevillea, and pepper trees along Euclid Avenue. We were exhausted, ecstatic, and in need of baths. I shared my farewell gift of lavender bath salts, and we emerged in turn, fragrant and ready to set up housekeeping. Lunch? Our Greyhound breakfasts still weighed on our stomachs. Our trunks were delivered, and we unpacked, dividing our meager wardrobes between a closet off the kitchen and the closet between the two rooms. Norma had brought an unexpected luxury, a small radio that we placed on the lamp table. She set photographs of her two handsome brothers on her half of the dressing table.

We placed a sign for the iceman in the front window before we walked to the A&P to lay in a supply of groceries. Then, groggy with fatigue, we prepared a hasty supper on the three-burners-over-an-oven stove and, like the good housekeepers our mothers had brought us up to be, washed and dried the dishes and returned them to the china cabinet.

By then we could barely stay awake, so we tackled the studio couch Mrs. Tuckness had bought for us to sleep on. She had explained, "When young men come to call, it wouldn't do to have a bed in the living room."

That green couch! It had three cushions propped against the wall. The bottom of the couch pulled out like a drawer to make a second place to sleep and for storing bedding during the day. We had to move the mattress from the top to the pull-out section. Because Norma was tall, she took the foundation of the couch, which had springs and was a few inches longer and about six inches higher than the lower half. When we made up our uneven bed with our new sheets, we discovered there was no place for Norma to tuck in her half of the bedding. "Never mind," she said. "I can balance the cushions on my feet to hold the blanket down."

Exhausted, I fell into my half of the bed and watched, fascinated, as Norma went through a series of exercises. That's a P.E. major for you, I thought. When she had completed her exercises, Norma climbed into bed, as exhausted as I, and balanced the green cushions on her feet. We both slept soundly.

In the morning we awoke to the song of a mockingbird. Because we were so happy, we lay in bed singing at the top of our voices a popular song: "You push the middle valve down. The music goes 'round and around, wo-ho-ho-ho, and comes out here!" We had actually made it back to Chaffey and one more year of college.

Life with a P.E. Major

The next afternoon, when Norma and I had recovered from the day before, someone knocked on our kitchen door. A strange man introduced himself, said he lived in a room at the rear of the house, and held out a basket of tomatoes. We were delighted, accepted them, thanked him, and closed the door. Late the next afternoon he knocked again and offered us the evening paper, which he could not have had time to read. Again we accepted his gift, thanked him, and shut the door. This went on for several days before he gave up and kept his paper. We were so naïve we did not realize that he expected to be invited in. After all, he was old. Probably thirty.

For two such different people, Norma and I got

along surprisingly well, although she said I made her feel tall and lanky, and I said she made me feel short and dumpy. We enjoyed housekeeping without our mothers telling us what to do even though we did exactly what they would have wanted us to.

The first one home from school shopped for groceries with money from the $7.50 apiece that we had deposited in a cookie jar for a month's supply of food. Sometimes, if our schedules permitted, we went to the A&P together because marketing was fun. The young men who worked there were lively and often stuck a thumb into an avocado. "Oops! Damaged goods. Can't sell that," they would say, and present it to us. Once when they marched up and down the aisles with brooms over their shoulders whistling "The Stars and Stripes Forever" for our amusement, the manager appeared. Suddenly the men were diligently sweeping while Norma and I examined the vegetables.

One joint attempt at washing sheets and towels in the laundry tub in the shed behind the house was enough for us. We sent our linens to a laundry and subtracted the money from the cookie jar. Every morning we walked to school with our dishes washed, our lunches packed, and our bed converted to a couch. Our mothers would have been proud.

The icebox somehow turned into my responsibility because Norma had a carefree attitude toward it. During the day she simply put it out of her mind. I could not. That icebox haunted me. Suddenly, in the middle of class, I would remember that we had forgotten to empty the pan under it that, at that very moment, might be overflowing and leaking through the floor onto Mrs. Tuckness's bed downstairs. Between classes I would rush to telephone her. She was always grateful for my warning.

That first semester our social life was limited. Paul came to see me a couple of times before he went off to his junior year at U.S.C. and a part-time job on the *Los Angeles Times*. We walked up Euclid Avenue to see the new Chaffey library and the new women's gym built with government funds. We talked about our futures and Paul revealed, without actually saying so, that even with a scholarship and a part-time job he had to manage on very little money. Once when Verna drove into Los Angeles to attend the book breakfast, I went along and met Paul to sit for a few minutes on a bench in Pershing Square before he had to go back to the *Times*. He looked tired. I wondered about his living conditions in Los Angeles but did not ask and did not expect to see him again. His work, our studies, and our lack of money, I knew, made meetings impossible. I was sorry, but our goals were more important than our friendship.

Sometimes Atlee and his friend Harold would drop in to listen to Norma's radio. Norma and I were always careful to walk around and to laugh heartily from time to time so Mrs. Tuckness would not be alarmed by silence overhead. Once the boys drove us to a movie in Pomona in the topless Rickenbacker. They sat in the front seat while we sat in the back with our hair tousled by the wind. They paid our admissions, but they refused to be seen sitting with us. What could we expect of sixteen-year-old boys?

The Clapps invited us to dinner and so did Norma's friends. Connie, a bright-eyed sparrow of a girl who was to be my friend all her life, often dropped in for supper after stopping at the A&P to buy "whatever meat the girls were having." In my *Argus* at the end of the year she reminded me of "dinners at your apartment when we could not eat for laughing." We went to football games in Connie's family car and to YWCA suppers where Norma and I were usually given leftover casserole dishes to take home. We went to school dances, Norma and I, each with somebody's brother, while Connie went with Park, a minister's son, whom she was pursuing and appeared to be gaining on.

One spring day, as I ate my lunch on Chaffey's lawn, I came to know a freshman, Frank, whom I treated with a touch of condescension because I assumed he was younger than I. At least, that was how he seemed after Gerhart and Paul until he admitted with amusement that he was a year older. His ambition was to become a politician, and he treated me with such formality that I felt I had to behave with unnatural dignity. This did not prevent us from having some pleasant times together. We went to a dance at the Red Hill Country Club, where he looked handsome in what every young man aspired to own, a white jacket, which I was pleased to be seen with, but Frank was tall, and I worried about smearing lipstick on his white shoulder as we danced. One day we drove in a borrowed car to Los Angeles to see *The Great Ziegfeld* at Grauman's Chinese Theatre and to admire the footprints of movie stars in concrete. Could Gloria Swanson's feet really have been that small? We finished the day with dinner at Lucca's—the first Italian meal I had ever eaten. I liked Frank but somehow could never get over feeling we were both pretending to be something we were not. Probably I was wrong and was only responding to Frank's natural reserve.

Norma had another source of recreation, which was exhilarating to her but would have been misery to me. These were Play Days, when she went off with a group of P.E. majors to other schools where they spent happy, for them, days of sports: baseball, archery, swimming, hockey, and tennis. Norma returned glowing with health and always went through her program of exercises while we listened to the news and I lay lazily on my low half of the couch. Norma followed events in Europe closely. She was afraid her brothers might have to go to war.

Norma studied at the kitchen table and solved math problems in ink on the oilcloth, which she scrubbed off before she went to bed. Now the icebox was her problem. The steady drip-drip of melting ice irritated her, so she put our dishcloth in the pan to muffle the drips, a nuisance because she had to fish it out, cold and sopping, before we could wash our breakfast dishes. Except when Atlee and Harold dropped in, I studied in the living-bedroom, sitting in the rocking chair with my feet up on the gas heater, which we never turned on.

We were both getting laboratory sciences "out of the way." Norma was studying zoology, which required dissecting a rabbit that she fished out of a barrel of formaldehyde on lab days. We joked about serving it for dinner when she finished dissecting it. While Norma was studying the anatomy of her pickled rabbit, I was studying botany because I had enjoyed the study of plants in my high school biology course. I was also taking psychology and two English courses from Mr. Palmer and two units of conversational French from Dr. Miller.

And then there was P.E. in the new women's gym, where the subject of scandalized talk was communal showers in one large room with showerheads along two sides. *There was no privacy,* people said. Like most gossip, this was not entirely true. There were several stall showers for modest maidens, but many girls adjusted the showerheads so that opposing streams of water met in the center of the room, sending spray in all directions. Then they raced up and down, spluttering and splashing, dancing and leaping like nymphs. I rarely used these showers because I didn't want to get my hair soaked.

My metatarsal arches must have improved because I was no longer required to pick up marbles with my toes. Instead, I was assigned to a folk dancing class, which I enjoyed. To this day, whenever I hear "La Cucaracha," I feel an urge to spring to my feet and, with my hands on my hips, stamp out imaginary cockroaches.

Of my courses, although I really did not count P.E., English Composition was the most absorbing. Mr. Palmer assigned us a daily three-hundred-word paper on any subject, to be poked through a slot in the locker nearest his office by three o'clock every school day. We were to do this until someone in the class earned an A. At first it was easy. I described the view from our kitchen window, the scene inside a shoe repair shop, my grandfather's store in Oregon, the sound of palm trees at night, but as the days went by, I began to feel as if I had written everything in the world there was to write about. Still Mr. Palmer hoarded his A's. I also began to think, but did not write, about myself in the third person: Her saddle shoes crushed pepper berries into the lawn as she walked under the feathery trees. She joined friends on the school steps, tore open her lunch bag, and bit into a peanut-butter sandwich. Bending over, she tightened the laces of her gym shoes and tied them in a neat bow before she . . .

Because I was also studying psychology, I began to wonder if I might lose my mind if this went on. Finally, *finally,* after what seemed like weeks, Mr. Palmer announced that an A paper had been turned in. It was mine, a description of a shabby old man shuffling through a restaurant trying to sell violets, a sad Depression scene I had witnessed when a young man named Bob had taken me to a Portland restaurant for a hamburger. People had money for hamburgers, but no one had money for violets. When Mr. Palmer read my melancholy description aloud, the class was grateful to me for commuting our sentence of a daily three hundred words.

One day, when five dollars arrived from my grandfather, I went into a shop to buy yarn to knit Norma a pair of bed socks for Christmas because the cushions balanced on her feet often fell off, exposing her toes to the chilly night air. Knitting was popular at Chaffey. When the shop owner learned that I could knit lace patterns, she asked me to take on the difficult parts of other customers' knitting. To be paid for something I enjoyed! I was delighted and knit lace yokes, for which I was paid seventy-five cents an ounce. Norma and I then decided to knit ourselves dresses out of raw silk yarn, but because we could not afford to buy all the yarn at once, the shop owner kept the skeins and allowed us to pay for them as needed. I knit along with other girls in classes, at YWCA meetings, and at tea at Dr. Miller's home, where we rummaged around in our minds for easy verbs to use in the required French conversation.

Then one day the Dean of Women called me in and asked if I had ever studied Latin. I had, for two years at Mother's insistence, "because Latin was the foundation of language." The dean offered me the task of correcting high school Latin papers. I was paid out of National Youth Administration funds for the boring work, which paid for the rest of my silk yarn.

My finances continued to improve. Alberta Schaeffer, the Ontario librarian, knocked on our door. "Mrs. Clapp recommended you for substitute work in the library. Would you be interested?" she asked. Would I! Of course I would. Miss Schaeffer cautioned me that the library board would fire without notice any librarian seen drinking or smoking in a public place. I did not find this a problem.

In 1935, in the Ontario library, any librarian who was ill had to pay a substitute out of her own pocket. Forty whole cents an hour. I didn't want to wish the librarians any hard luck, but I enjoyed working at the circulation desk of the old Carnegie library. One elderly woman was indignant because *pitchblende* was not in the encyclopedia. Having met the word in Geology, I found it easily; she had not realized it was spelled with a *t*. Then Miss Schaeffer asked if I could translate a letter from France, which the local nursery, noted for citrus plants, had received. The letter in simple business French was easy to translate, and I was elated to have used both geology and French in real life while earning money in a library. Patrons furnished subjects for English compositions. An old man who spent most of his days in the library confided that he called it his private club. Describing him earned me another A. During the year I banked my earnings, most of them from an unfortunate librarian who suffered a bad case of trench mouth. Fifty dollars! I would not go into the future empty-handed.

The future was a worry to most Chaffey students. Norma, whose brothers were graduating in June, planned to go with hockey stick and tennis racquet to Washington State to continue P.E. Many were applying for scholarships at the University of Southern California. Others hoped to go to Cal, as the University of California at Berkeley was called by everyone before other campuses were built and it became known as U.C., Berkeley. Everyone was filling out applications, so I filled out one, too. Although I had no hope of going there, I applied to Cal because of its graduate School of Librarianship, an application to fantasy. How could I possibly manage three years of attendance at a university that charged $150 a year in nonresident tuition?

Connie and I were both accepted by Cal, with my acceptance stipulating that I must take one year of either philosophy or mathematics. When I wrote this news in my weekly letter home, Mother answered that she and Dad had talked it over and decided that somehow they could manage the nonresident tuition. I learned later that my father, like many Depression fathers, borrowed on his life insurance.

There was, however, another obstacle: living. Because Oregon friends all lived in dormitories or sorority houses, I had assumed that all college women lived this way, which I knew I could not afford. I soon learned from others that most Cal students had to find their own living accommodations. Five of us talked about renting an apartment. Norma and I got along, with one or two rough patches, but five girls with different allowances, temperaments, interests, and schedules? I was dubious.

The news of cooperative houses at Cal filtered down by way of former Chaffey students, mostly brothers, for in the 1930s when money was hard to come by, many parents felt it was more important to educate their sons, who would have to support families, than their daughters, who would be supported by husbands. First we heard of cooperative houses for men: Barrington and Sheridan. Then we learned that in January of that year a women's cooperative, Stebbins Hall, had been established. Room and board were eighteen dollars a month plus half an hour of work a day. I began to be hopeful, but the catch, I soon learned via rumor, was a waiting list so long there was no point in applying so late in the year. Still . . .

Worrying about living conditions would do no good, so as Mother so often advised, I took one day at a time. Except for Dr. Miller's spoiling Christmas vacation by requiring us to read *Madame Bovary* without a dictionary, the winter days, most of them, were passing happily by, interrupted by another phenomenon, almost as interesting as an earthquake. One night the notorious Santa Ana winds began to blow in from the desert. Pepper trees tossed their tousled heads, and palm fronds danced and rattled. As the winds increased, we closed all our windows and went through our usual bedtime ritual of Norma doing her exercises, putting our hair up on curlers, and listening to the news while Norma worried about her brothers.

Then we climbed into our uneven, uncomfortable bed, but that night we slept very little. The winds increased. We felt as if we were breathing dust and our skins were drying up. We pulled the sheet over our noses. The grevillea twisted, branches broke off, clattering palm fronds were ripped away, trash cans bounced down the street. We were afraid the windows were going to blow in. Finally, when daylight came and the winds calmed, we dragged ourselves out of bed. Everything was covered with dust, and under the closed kitchen window sand was a quarter of an inch deep. Good housekeepers that we were, we cleaned it all up before we left for school, and I had another subject for a composition.

And then the first semester grades came out. I leafed through the report slips, found more A's than I really expected, even an A– in Conversational French, which was kindness on Dr. Miller's part, a B– in P.E., but who cared? And then D in Botany, a terrible shock. A D! No one gave me D's, not even P.E. teachers. It simply wasn't done, I felt, because along the path of education several teachers had told their classes that they didn't want to hear any complaints about grades because what went into our heads was more important than a grade. I believed them. I worked hard at subjects that interested me, was satisfied with disgraceless B's in others, and didn't care what I got in P.E. But a D! I would be drummed out of the honor society. The humiliation was too much to bear.

I accosted Mr. Stanford after class. Why had he given me a D? "Because that is what you earned," he said. I stopped and thought. There was that exam question that required us to identify samples of wood and tell how they had been sawed. I had been surprised by the question and guessed at the answers. Then there were my struggles with the microscope. I wasn't very good at using it. Mr. Stanford insisted the proper way was to look through the microscope with one eye and use the other eye for drawing what we saw. I usually gave up, looked back and forth with both eyes, and emerged from the lab feeling seasick.

No one else reeled out of the lab pale with nausea. Then I recalled that I was unable to see trees, visible to everyone else, on the mountains, so I wrote home saying I needed glasses. Mother's reply was prompt and definite. Rather than wear glasses, I was to drop out of school and come home. Never! I said no more about my eyesight.

As I stood before Mr. Stanford, I must have looked so humbled that he told me that if I raised my grade the second semester, he would average the two semester grades and give me one grade for the year. I thanked him, determined I would manage an A.

In pursuit of that A I found a useful pamphlet called *How to Study* that advised spaced repetition and reviewing work at bedtime for subjects requiring memorization. I lugged my botany text around and went over memory work several times a day. At bedtime, while Norma exercised her body, I exercised my mind on botany.

My test grades shot up, but that left my microscope problem. I shared the microscope with a young man, Said Shaheen, who had come from Palestine to study citriculture. As I frowned through the lens, he asked me if I was "stuck up."

Surprised, I answered, "I hope not."

"Perhaps I can help," he offered.

Then I realized he meant "stuck," not "stuck up." Together we struggled on, he with his idioms, I with the microscope.

That second semester we were to find and identify a collection of wildflowers. But where was I to find wildflowers? Atlee came to my rescue in his Rickenbacker. We drove out into the desert, where he steered with one hand, and, keeping our eyes out for flowers, we both leaned out open doors. If either of us saw a flower, he stopped while I jumped out and picked it.

Identifying desert flowers was difficult for an

Oregonian. Other students knew what they were aiming for before they started. I struggled, wishing I were studying botany in Oregon, where I was familiar with the trilliums, Johnny-jump-ups, and lady slippers of Oregon woods and pastures, and hoping the little brown book, the key to flowers, would lead me to the right answer. My semester grade was A, the D was expunged from my record, my grade for the year was B+, and I no longer felt I was in disgrace. I had learned a lesson more valuable than botany. The whole experience was humbling.

The second pitfall on the path to higher learning was the second semester of P.E. While Norma cavorted in the sunshine with hockey stick or badminton racquet, I was assigned to a tap-dancing class with other girls who would never leave their mark on the world on the playing fields of Chaffey. To borrow words from Ruth Tremaine Kegley's freshman drama class, I "hated, detested, abominated, and despised" tap dancing. At the end of the semester Mrs. Quackenbush announced that each of us was required to compose an original tap dance for our final examination.

A final in P.E., how ridiculous, I thought as rebellion rose within me. After class I approached Mrs. Quackenbush and asked, "What will happen if I don't compose a tap dance?"

She promptly squashed my small rebellion. "Then you won't graduate," she said.

I fumed. When no one was looking, I tried to compose a tap dance, but I was no Ginger Rogers. Neither was I Shirley Temple tapping down the stairs with Bill Robinson. I was plain old me with feet heavy with resistance. On what I thought of as execution day, still not knowing how I was going to come up with an original tap dance, I borrowed a pair of tap shoes that made a reassuring clackety-clack as I walked across the gym floor. Grimly I waited my turn while other girls went through their neat composed routines. My name was called, I asked the pianist to play "A Little Bit Independent," took a deep breath, gritted my teeth, sacrificed my integrity, and hopped, stepped, brushed, and slapped down in no particular pattern. Finally the pianist stopped. "Good," said Mrs. Quackenbush, but I didn't believe she was referring to my dancing. Oh well. At least I passed P.E. with a semester grade of B–.

Years later I met a tall, somewhat awkward woman who had been given the same assignment at another junior college and refused to go through with it. She did not graduate and never finished college.

While I dragged my feet in P.E., I was eager to attempt the last assignment in English Composition, a short story. My trouble was I couldn't think of a plot, and in those days a short story was supposed to have a plot. I thought and thought. I had lived in several settings, known a variety of people, and had a good memory for dialogue, but I could not hatch a plot.

Finally I sat down in the rocking chair, placed my feet on the gas heater, and commanded myself: Write! The first thing that came to mind was my wretched experience in the first grade when I was learning to read. I turned myself into a third-person child, miserable and frightened in the reading circle, who in desperation mispronounced *city,* calling it *kitty* even though she knew it was wrong. I wrote of the snickers of the class, the harshness of the teacher. But where was my plot? I finally fabricated an ending having the teacher ask if anyone could tell a story, something my own teacher would not have done. My timid alter ego volunteered, stood before the class, and told a folktale her mother had read to her many times. The class listened, the teacher praised her, and my story had a happy ending. Mr. Palmer gave me an unqualified A, read my story to the class, and said, "This story is nothing to be ashamed of," lighting me with joy with this, for him, lavish praise. Without knowing it, I had begun to write the story of my life.

The semester was ending. Yearbooks were exchanged. Norma wrote a word or two beside every picture of herself. "Nut!" under the class picture, and beside others, "Roomy," "Athlete!" "What again!" "Yes me!" Norma was no sentimentalist.

Connie wrote an honest, tender letter telling me I had been sweet to her when she didn't deserve it. She hoped I was her friend for life (I was) and that I would be "one true friend, who would sympathize and understand."

Frank wrote a somewhat pompous message telling me I was "too perfect" and that I "would be a wonderful wife for a politician. You have every charm and quality that such a woman needs. This is not a proposal—just an explanation." He closed his message with "Love" and a footnote: "Love—Strong liking *(sic)*. The state of feeling kindly toward others." Such caution was quite unnecessary.

As the semester drew to a close, days passed much too fast. Norma's parents drove down from Washington to see us, in our gray caps and gowns, receive our Associate of Arts diplomas.

The next morning Norma and I climbed into the backseat of her parents' car. We were both sad to leave Ontario, but this time I did not shed tears. I was going, as Mother would say, "by hook or by crook" to Cal even if I had to live under a bush, but I wanted to remember every geranium and pepper tree, the brown mountains, and Chaffey's tower against the blue sky.

"Chaffey, where the fronded palm uplifted to the sky .

Virginia gives Guard a bath.

Atlee hugs Guard.

P.E. teacher, fifty-three, and son, nineteen, flex their muscles.

Beverly after gaining weight eating avocados, Verna, Virginia, Mother Clapp, and Fred

Claudine reads her mail at "Jessica Todd Hell."

Posing prettily in pink with my junior college yearbook

Peeking out the door of the Ontario apartment. Buildings often went without fresh paint during the Depression.

Norma on the balcony outside our apartment on Euclid Avenue, Ontario

Connie at U.S.C., where she was enticed by a larger scholarship than that offered by Cal

Cooperation

On the drive up the coast Norma's parents offered to stop in Berkeley for an hour so I could
visit Stebbins Hall. Inside Sather Gate, I consulted a map, raced across the campus up Euclid
Avenue and Ridge Road to arrive, flushed, pant-
ing, and with a stitch in my side, at the granite
steps of Stebbins Hall, a three-story L-shaped
building with a one-story dining room in the
angle of the L. The house-mother, an elderly
woman who walked with a cane, came to the door
and asked me to sit down before she explained
that there was no possibility of my being admitted for the fall semester. My look of despair and
disappointment must have touched her because
she kindly said that she would add my name to

the waiting list even though there were rarely any cancellations. Perhaps another semester . . .

I thanked the housemother, then, feeling that I should say something more, added that if I should be accepted, I hoped I would be assigned a roommate who was a good student and who did not smoke. In the 1930s many girls took up smoking as soon as they went away to college. Then I raced back across the campus to meet Norma and her parents and continue the drive home.

Summer vacation was mercifully short because Cal's fall semester began the middle of August. I read and reread the dean's list of approved housing, which listed nothing I could afford and which I did not show my parents, who seemed not to give a thought as to how I would live. I had to manage somehow, even if I had to work for my room and board. I saw my friends, made over some clothes, and at Mother's suggestion made a dark red taffeta formal and a rose moiré dress with three black velvet bands around the hem for parties Mother was sure I would be invited to. Mother also saw to it that I had a beautiful tailor-made coat. I wish I still had it.

The best part of summer was a couple of weekends spent at Puddin' with Claudine and her mother. Claudine had been hired to teach first and second grades in Dee, a sawmill town near Mount Hood. She was to earn seventy-five dollars a month for nine months plus an extra five dollars a month because she could play the piano. Eighty dollars a month and she would no longer live at home! Lucky Claudine. My own financial independence required two more years of college and a year of graduate work, which seemed forever when compared with the riches Claudine was soon to earn with her brand-new credential.

Then one sunny afternoon late in July the mailman shoved a letter through the mail slot, and Mother, always an eager mailbox watcher, opened the little door in the living room wall, pulled out an envelope, glanced at it, and handed it to me. The leaping heart of Wordsworth beholding a rainbow in the sky could not compare with the leaping of my heart when I beheld a letter from Stebbins Hall. I had been accepted for the fall semester. Joy flooded through me. Now I had nothing to worry about, not a single thing. I danced around, waving the letter.

Mother, who could always find something to worry her, said, "You must not let Stebbins make you wait on table. Once a waitress, always a waitress."

Dad, when he came home from work and heard the news, said I had had enough of travel by

Greyhound. I must travel by train and sleep in a berth. Mother gave me precise instructions on how to button the green curtains that would enclose the berth, how to go to the dining car, how to tip the porter. Train travel was more comfortable but less interesting than bus travel. The Pullman car was half-empty, and I had no one to talk to. Eating the cheapest meal in the dining car with its starched napkins and rosebuds in silver vases gave me an agreeable feeling of sophistication in spite of an awkward encounter with a catsup bottle that refused to yield its contents until the waiter gave it a whack.

And so, one August morning as the fog was retreating from San Francisco Bay, I disembarked Southern Pacific into a world that smelled like tomato catsup. That's peculiar, I thought as I looked up University Avenue toward the Campanile, why should a university smell like catsup? As I collected my steamer trunk and typewriter crate, I felt academically confident. In spite of the expunged D in Botany, I had always been an honor student. In many other ways, however, I felt insecure. Did I have enough money, were my clothes right, would I make friends, would I choose the right courses? The great University loomed large and exciting, a new field to conquer.

At Stebbins I was given a key and shown to room 228 at the rear of the building, a room I was to occupy for two of the most interesting years of my life. It overlooked a row of garages with clotheslines on the roofs. Beyond, a weedy hill slanted up to the backs of small apartment houses. The room had cream-colored walls and curtains, basic furniture, and, I noted with interest, a wall telephone, which I was to learn could receive incoming calls. Outgoing calls were made on a pay phone on the stair landing. The room was part of a suite, connected by a bathroom to another room.

When I had finished unpacking, the work-shift manager knocked on the door and told me I had been assigned to wash glassware after lunch. Would Mother approve, I wondered as I made up my bed with its terra-cotta-colored spread. Then I sat down to write a note to my parents telling them I had arrived safely and would not be waiting tables. To be on the safe side, I did not mention what I would be doing.

When I returned from mailing my note, I found my roommate had arrived and was unpacking. Her name was Miriam. She was a tall, slender girl with curly hair who was wearing blue shorts and a pink blouse. We exchanged fundamental roommate information. She was a sophomore from Utah and was putting herself through Cal on a scholarship awarded each year to the Utah student with the highest grade point average. She had won it twice and had every intention of winning it two more years. At Stebbins she chose to wait on tables at dinner because waitresses ate before the other girls. This allowed her to go to the library early.

"I'm so glad you're here," Miriam told me. "My last roommate tried to keep a puppy in the bathroom."

Miriam's wardrobe, as limited as mine, was quickly unpacked. She tacked her shoe bag above mine on the closet door. Stebbins had a rule that nothing was allowed on closet floors or under beds. Then she set about making up her bed as if the foot were the head, placed her pillow at the opposite end, and covered her bed with the spread so our beds looked alike.

How odd. "Why do you make your bed that way?" I asked.

"The dean says we have to sleep with our heads eight feet apart, and the only way we can do it is for one of us to sleep with her head at the foot of the bed."

Diagonally our heads were eight feet apart. Maybe that's Cal's way of preventing the spread of germs, I thought.

Then Miriam made an astonishing remark. "Someday I'm going to marry a physicist."

To me physics was a course in a catalog. I had never given the subject a thought, other than to avoid it. "Any special physicist?" I asked.

"No."

"Then why a physicist?"

"Because they are so nice," she answered. "I am sure one will come along someday."

I could see that I had an unusual roommate.

While Miriam and I were getting to know each other, the house was filled with thumps of trunks and boxes, and the laughter and greeting of girls, all sorts of girls, I was to learn in the next few days. Tall, short, shy, "fast," brilliant, struggling, colorless, beautiful, neat, sloppy, confident, brokenhearted. Most were wearing homemade clothes. One girl had tailored a coat from a blanket. They came from small towns, ranches, medium-sized cities outside commuting distance of Oakland and San Francisco, and other states. Girls from small high schools were confused and bewildered in a university of more than fourteen thousand students. Many girls had no idea of the sort of education they wanted or needed. Sheltered girls were overwhelmed by the freedom of a university that expected them to be adults. Some girls knew exactly where they were going in life and how they would get there. Some, and I was one, were sure where they wanted to go but did not know if they could find the money to get there.

A few girls were ashamed of living in a cooperative house, but most were glad to be there. Some had had unsatisfactory experiences working for room and board even though the university set the pay and the number of hours worked. Fitting into a strange household was awkward, and they were usually expected to baby-sit weekends when they longed for fun. One girl had been treated as a maid and required to wear a little white apron and a cap. For them Stebbins was a relief.

During the two years I lived at Stebbins, four girls occupied the other half of the suite at different times. One was a statuesque girl from Carmel who had worked as an artists' model. "Naked?" I asked, shocked.

"Oh yes," she answered, and made a face. She had not enjoyed the work.

Another girl, short and plump, suffered because she felt she was too fat. Sometimes when I came in from classes, I would find her, florid and sweating, wrapped in a woolen blanket, lying on her bed after soaking herself in bathwater as hot as she could stand. Her weight loss, if any, was only temporary, and to me did not seem worth the misery, but then I was, as people often said, "just skin and bones."

Then there was a girl from Montana who padded around in beaded moccasins. Her roommate was tall, beautiful Nellie, who once came to me in desperation. She had been elected to the history honor society and was told that for her initiation she was required to read an original poem about the War of Jenkins' Ear. Since I was an English major, would I *please* write it for her? I did not fancy myself a poet but was willing to try if she would tell me what the battle was about. She told me about the eighteenth-century battle between England and Spain that began with Captain Jenkins displaying in the House of Commons his ear, which had been amputated by Spaniards before they pillaged his ship. This colorful event seemed to lend itself to the ballad form, and so, tapping out rhythm with my pencil, I wrote "The Ballad of Jenkins' Ear." Nellie reported that it was well received at the dinner. I wish I had kept a copy.

These four suite-mates, all so different, shared one thing in common: Each took her turn at cleaning the bathroom without complaint. In addition to our bathroom-cleaning schedule, roommates took turns dusting furniture, vacuuming rugs, and making sure there were no dust mice under beds or on closet floors. All rooms were inspected once a week. Slovenliness was not acceptable at Stebbins Hall.

I spent the first day or two of that first semester hurrying up and down hills, campus map in hand, inhaling the smell of tomato catsup, which someone had explained came from a cannery "down in the flats." Downhill to Harmon Gym, where I waited in a long, long line to register for classes, uphill to the women's gym for a physical examination. There all the girls were handed ancient gray bathing suits to wear for modesty. Why I cannot guess. They were ill-fitting and all had large holes in the crotches. Off to Cowell Hospital for a hearing test, but I do not recall an eye test. Downhill again to register at the Employment Office, which had nothing to offer someone who had earned money only by knitting or by working in a library. New students did not rate even the most menial job of shelving books. With ravenous appetite I hurried back up the hill to Stebbins while music rang out from the Campanile, making my feet lighter as they carried me toward food.

Meals at Stebbins! Eighty-two girls plus fifteen boarders who lived in rooming houses across the street. The low ceiling of our crowded dining room compressed conversation, laughter, and the rattle of dishes into a din that forced us to raise our voices to high pitches as if we were talking to people who had hearing problems. Waitresses hurried, balancing as many as five plates at a time. Busgirls leaned to one side under the weight of heavy trays of dirty dishes they were carrying to the kitchen. Nevertheless, from the babble I learned that at Cal grades were important, and something to worry about. Required courses were often dreaded and certain professors should be avoided if possible. When I shouted my name and "I'm majoring in English," I was surprised at the sort of answers shouted back: "Poor you" or "I'm glad I'm not in your shoes. You get to take English Comprehensive!" What's so terrible about an English exam, I wondered. Their remarks stayed with me as I joined another girl in the kitchen to attack glassware.

We filled two sinks with hot water, poured into one strong granulated soap that made us sneeze. We came to dread days when sherbet glasses doubled our work, but we felt our job was better than that of girls who scraped plates and loaded them into the antique dishwasher. We worked as fast as we could, entertaining ourselves with knock-knock jokes, and left the kitchen damp with perspiration and with hands that looked like wet pink corduroy. The luxury of rubber gloves did not enter our frugal minds.

After my first day of glass washing, I ran upstairs to consult my copy of the General Catalogue and read in the English section, "The Comprehensive Final Examination must be taken at the end of the senior year. It will consist of two three-hour papers, the second of which will take the form of an essay. The examination will cover English literature from 1350 to 1900." There goes Beowulf, I thought. He would be no help at all. Neither would the modern American poetry, biography, or essays I had enjoyed at Chaffey. Mrs. Kegley's course in drama, although called English, had been mostly about playwrights of other countries. I consulted the lower-division courses taught at Cal, which included Survey of English Literature, which I had not had, at least not as described in the catalog. Somehow I would have to manage.

I soon put the Comprehensive out of my mind because of the struggle going on at Stebbins Hall. Almost as soon as the semester began, girls began to mutter with dissatisfaction over the food. Menus were planned by the housemother, who sat erect at the head table with her mouth set in a straight line. Plainly, she expected us to eat without complaint the meals set before us. Since food had never particularly interested me,

I was not much concerned until the day stewed rabbit was served. The rabbit had been shot. We knew this because we found shot in the meat. And then there was a lunch of inedible, lightly scorched oyster soup with cantaloupe for dessert. Hungry girls who burned energy climbing hills and stairs pushed their dishes away while the housemother sat erect, eating her scorched soup as if she savored it. Madeline, the student manager, a young woman of intelligence and character, rose from the table and headed for the office of the Dean of Women while the rest of us faced a hungry afternoon.

The housemother was soon replaced. Although I was not sorry to see her go, I always suspected she had moved me ahead on the waiting list because I had requested a roommate who was a good student and who did not smoke. Such virtue would have appealed to her.

A new housemother arrived, Mrs. Ruth Cochran. She was young, sympathetic, and understanding of the times in which we lived. She also understood that we lived in a cooperative house run by students and not by the housemother. She did oversee menus, which the cook prepared with food purchased cooperatively with the two men's houses and adapted to the appetites of active young women. Unlike students who lived in boardinghouses, we enjoyed the luxury of an egg for Sunday breakfast.

The second semester, I felt I had had my share of corduroy hands and managed to get transferred to the switchboard. This work shift required an hour a day because theoretically operators could study while on duty. In practice, study was almost impossible because of interruptions: plugging in the lines for incoming calls, pulling levers to ring bells, looking over young men as I rang their dates' rooms to announce them. If the man was a blind date, the girl would usually whisper, "How does he look?" If the man had gone into the living room to wait, I could whisper, "Nice," "So-so," "Tall," "Short," or whatever word I could find to help the girl meet her evening's fate.

Calls for baby-sitters were passed on to any girl I knew who was in real need of money. One call I kept for myself, for as much as I enjoyed my noisy life at Stebbins, a quiet evening in an unusual house in the hills was a treat. This house was built around a circular staircase, and every room was on a different level. The well-behaved little girl, Donna, went to bed early but sometimes called out, "Miss Bunn, I want a dwink of water." Running around the staircase with a glass of water was the only interruption in peaceful, comfortable evenings in a quiet living room with a view of the lights of San Francisco. As I absorbed the soothing silence, I felt the Berkeley Hills must be the loveliest spot in the world and longed to live there myself someday.

My senior year I became house secretary, a position that relieved me of a work shift but required that I take minutes of compulsory monthly house meetings and post them on the bulletin board. These meetings were usually short because everyone was anxious to get to the library. The house president made announcements: "Please do not linger over good-nights. Necking on the front steps gives Stebbins a bad name." To my surprise, for several years afterward, whenever I met someone who had lived at Stebbins, she often said, "Oh, you're the one who wrote those hilarious minutes." Hilarious? I wasn't trying to be funny. I simply recorded what took place. Years later, when I read a statement by James Thurber, "Humor is best that lies closest to the familiar," I began to understand.

Council meetings went on much longer—too long, we felt, if we had papers due or tests the next day. These meetings dealt with more serious matters, often individual behavior, and minutes were not posted for all to read. A major problem was the Dean of Women, who felt we should cut expenses by eliminating the switchboard, which cost what now seems like a ridiculously small amount, something like twenty-eight dollars a month for all of Stebbins. Never, we vowed, would we part with the switchboard. If we could not receive incoming calls, how could men get in touch with us? Then there was the problem of the girl who wore slacks to the library. It was agreed she be told that slacks were inappropriate for wear outside the house. And what about the girl who was conspicuously pregnant but behaved as if she hadn't noticed? Should she be allowed to remain at Stebbins? Someone pointed out that people were saying, "You see what comes out of Stebbins Hall." Although we all felt we had our good reputation to maintain, we decided, after long and serious discussion, that the girl should stay. We would say nothing. She needed us no matter what others said about the virtue, or lack of virtue, of the residents of Stebbins Hall.

At the beginning of my second semester the house manager announced that the eighteen dollars a month we had been paying did not cover "depreciation of fixed assets." Our fee must therefore be raised to twenty-four dollars a month. We were aghast. Where could we find an additional six dollars a month when most of us could barely manage eighteen? Some girls felt they would have to drop out of school (as far as I know none did); others reluctantly wrote home for money, something I refused to do. One girl had a white fur "bunny" jacket that she rented for fifty cents an evening to girls going to formal dances. It shed on dark suits. Some found odd jobs typing or baby-sitting. I was a poor typist, and baby-sitting, except for my one customer, was too time-consuming. Where could I find another six dollars?

I found six dollars in the style of the times. Hems twelve inches from the floor were no longer fashionable, so I opened a skirt-shortening business: fifty cents a skirt if it was straight and didn't have pleats. I could shorten a straight skirt in half to three-quarters of an hour, which beat the forty cents an hour Cal set for student labor, and I saved precious time because I could work in my room. My business, although hardly flourishing, did bring in enough to make up the six dollars without my having to write home for money, something I had vowed I would never do. I wanted independence more than anything.

Fun at Cal

At the beginning of the semester, on late sunny afternoons, some of us ran up the hill to the Pacific School of Religion to play a children's game, statue, on the lawn. Other times, after dinner, when we had written "Libe" in the sign-out book, we went off to the library singing,

> "Ta-rootity-too, ta-rootity-toot!
> We are the girls from the institute.
> We do not smoke, we do not chew,
> We do not do what the other girls do!"

When the library closed at ten o'clock, we returned to Stebbins, most of us to continue studying.

Saturday afternoons the atmosphere of Stebbins changed. We washed our hair, and sometimes I cut Miriam's, which was so curly mistakes didn't show. We exchanged shoe polish and pressed our dresses in the basement laundry. Many of us chose the time before dinner to answer letters.

Next to Mother, my most loyal correspondent was Claudine, who wrote cheerful letters from the cold mill town fourteen miles from Mount Hood. Sometimes she enclosed a dollar bill in her letter. A whole dollar to spend any way I pleased! I bought silk stockings for special occasions, stockings without runs stopped by dabs of nail polish. Once I used Claudine's dollar to take a ferry trip to San Francisco, where I enjoyed a quiet, solitary lunch in a tearoom. Quiet and solitude were as precious as money when I lived at Stebbins.

With letters written, hair washed, and dresses pressed, we were ready for fun. Miriam had a number of male friends. Occasionally I went out with one, and once we double-dated, a memorable evening because one of the men had a car. We drove across the new San Francisco-Oakland Bay Bridge, something every student longed to do, for this bridge that we had seen being built was now open for traffic. The sodium-vapor lights shone down upon us, turning our complexions green and our dresses hideous colors, the sort of colors children mix from their paint boxes. Looking like specters did not dim our excitement at riding eight miles over water. In San Francisco we danced, without much enthusiasm as I recall, in the Colonial Room at the St. Francis Hotel, or "Frantic," as students usually called it. After waffles at Tiny's we drove back to Berkeley. I cannot recall a thing about the two men who were our escorts. They could not compare with the excitement of riding across the new bridge, even though the lights made us look like ghouls.

Campus social life centered on dances: club dances, house dances, fraternity and sorority dances. I was taken to one dance in a fraternity house that I found so boring—all that beer drinking—that I simply walked out and went back to Stebbins alone. Largest of all were the biweekly Assembly Dances held in Harmon Gym, admission fifteen cents with a student-body card, dates not necessary. Sometimes Miriam and I went, promising each other we would return to Stebbins together. The orchestras were good, and because Cal had two and a half male students to every female, there was always a stag line of men looking women over as if we were auditioning for the honor of dancing with them, which I suppose we were. I seemed to attract engineering students, all of them looking tired and overworked, some with slide rules (referred to by Stebbins girls as "sly drools") in their shirt pockets, which indicated they had dropped in for a breather before going back to their books, belying the campus myth that engineering students entered the Engineering Building and were not seen for four years. All of the engineers were serious, and we had little to talk about as we tried not to tread upon each other's toes. I never once met an engineering student at an Assembly Dance who was cheerful or a good dancer. As they concentrated on their feet, they seemed to have the weight of future bridges and skyscrapers on their shoulders. Apparently they recover from the oppression of the School of Engineering after graduation. Since college I have met a number of interesting engineers who, although they were serious men, could talk, laugh, and even dance like anyone else.

At one Assembly Dance a tall, thin young man with black hair and blue eyes stepped out of the stag line and asked me to dance. He said his name was Clarence Cleary. "Cleary?" I asked, never having heard the name. "How do you spell it?" He spelled it. He was from Sacramento. So were several Stebbins girls whom he knew, which gave us something in common. I hoped he would telephone me, and I was glad I was wearing a becoming pink dress Mother had made with great care and sent to me a few days before, a dress I found touching because Mother disliked sewing and was usually careless in her work.

In the meantime Miriam received a letter from a friend, a physics professor at the University of Washington, telling her a British physicist in this country on a Commonwealth Fellowship would be at Cal working with Dr. Ernest Lawrence and would call on her. Miriam hoped he would, and sure enough, Wilfrid called in person. He was handsome, very British, and was immediately entranced by Miriam.

Through Wilfrid I met several Commonwealth Fellows whose stipends must have been generous, for they had cars and seemed to have plenty of spending money. Wilfrid's roommate was Campbell, a chemist from Scotland who had once worked in a coal mine. We went as a group to Faculty Club dances, a dinner at the home of a professor, to Harmon Gym to hear George Gershwin play *Rhapsody in Blue* with the San Francisco Symphony. "Dreadful," pronounced Wilfrid.

Another time Miriam and I went with Fellows to see the cyclotron housed in a shack on the campus. I remember we had to take off our watches before we approached the invention where atoms were smashed to produce new radioactive species. The cyclotron was the reason Wilfrid was at Cal. All I knew about atoms I had learned in Philosophy 5A from studying Lucretius, an ancient Roman philosopher, who got it all wrong. I kept still and tried to look impressed by the strangely shaped device. If I had understood what the smashing of atoms would lead to, I would have been genuinely impressed and probably frightened.

Only once did I think of myself as going out on a date with a Fellow, an Oxford graduate and, as I recall, also a physicist. His dancing was as bad as or even worse than that of any undergraduate engineering student, or perhaps the English danced differently. When we were not dancing, I eluded his clutching hands. For some reason the Fellows left the Faculty Club dance early to go to another dance, in the Hotel Oakland, a place that was to play an important part in my life half a dozen years later. The ride to Oakland was harrowing. My date, fresh from England, drove on the left-hand side of the street while I clutched the door in fright. We rode over round metal buttons that protected streetcar riders from traffic as they boarded streetcars. Some people had to jump out of his way as we bumpety-bumped past.

I was relieved when what I had come to think of as the mad Englishman returned me safely but unnerved to Stebbins. He telephoned the next evening, but I told him I was much too busy to see him. He did not telephone again and probably thought of me as too American to appreciate an Englishman.

Clarence called, and so did other men. One I had met at the Masonic Club, which my parents arranged for me to join so I would "meet nice people." His name was Jack, and he was a graduate student in entomology. I went out with him two or three times, but somehow my intuition told me not to trust him, probably because he never asked me more than a day ahead. His explanation was that he was on call for inspecting incoming ships for foreign insects, an explanation that seemed logical after my bus experience at the California border. Nevertheless, I once said something about his being a bachelor and added, "But are you a bachelor?"

Jack laughed and said, "Where do you get such ideas in your pretty little head?" Having a pretty little head struck me as so ridiculous it was funny, but I managed not to laugh. To this day, when I do something stupid, I blame it on my pretty little head.

One night at an Assembly Dance, where I had

gone with Miriam, Jack stepped out of the stag line. As we were about to join the throng circulating the gym, a thin, tired-looking older woman interrupted and said to me, "I think we should know one another. I'm Jack's wife."

I was too numb with embarrassment and humiliation to say anything. There followed a bit of dialogue etched in my memory forever. Jack's wife said to her husband, "What do you see in her anyway?" Indignation erased my embarrassment.

He said, "She's young and fresh and there's a shine about her."

His wife snapped, "Don't worry. Men will take it off!" and stalked away.

Jack turned to me and said, "Believe me, Beverly, I wasn't making a play for you. Can't we talk this over?"

"No," I said, and walked away with tears of anger in my eyes.

In this assortment of social life there was Clarence. He was six years older than I and was putting himself through Cal by working part-time in the Bedding and Linen Department at Breuner's Furniture Store in Oakland. We went to a couple of Assembly Dances and ate bacon-and-tomato sandwiches and drank milk at the Jolly Roger. He was kind, gentle, quiet, and, best of all, single. I made sure of that. By now I was wise enough to go to the lobby of Cal Hall to consult a card file of students filled out when we registered. At the time I had wondered why we had to give our marital status. Now I knew.

Clarence, authentic bachelor, began to telephone me every afternoon at five before he left work, and I began to look forward to his calls. He was the middle of five children, and his mother, a widow, was a nurse in the emergency room of Sacramento Hospital. After junior college, and a series of low-paying jobs, whatever he could find in Depression times, he had returned to school at the California College of Agriculture in Davis, a sixteen-mile hitchhike from Sacramento. Drivers were kind to students. In two years, he was late for class only once. His interest was veterinary science, but he felt he should no longer live at home when his mother had younger children to support, so he became a dairy technician because he could earn a certificate in two years. He had worked for a dairy in Palo Alto, an experience that left him critical of ice cream. "Too much air incorporated into the mixture," he often commented when we bought ice-cream cones. As the Depression deepened, he had been laid off and decided to return to school. He was studying economics and history.

Men did not make up all of my social life. One

of the Stebbins girls stood out. I noticed her the first week of the semester at lunchtime when she bused heavy trays of dishes from the dining room to the kitchen. She was small, attractive, and wearing a becoming red-and-white-checked dress obviously made from a tablecloth, which suggested she was a girl of originality, initiative, and independence. Her name was Jane Chourré, and we soon became friends, lifelong friends, as it turned out. Jane was calmer and better organized than I and aspired to become a teacher. "Teaching is an honorable profession," she often said. "A teacher has a respected place in the community."

English was her major, and we shared several of the same classes. She often went home weekends and returned with begonias in vibrant colors, yellow, red, orange, and apricot, which her father grew as a hobby. If she was too busy to go home, her mother sometimes mailed her begonias, with each stem carefully secured in a balloon of water. Fresh flowers meant a lot at Stebbins. Mrs. Chourré understood this.

Jane invited me to spend Thanksgiving vacation with her in Mill Valley. Jane's parents were an unusual couple for those days, for Mrs. Chourré was both older and taller than her husband. Their children—Jane's sister, Marianne, and her brothers, Bud and Dick—were close in age because, as Mrs. Chourré put it matter-of-factly, "We wanted four children, and because I was older, we had to have them close together." She had been a home economics teacher and was always serene in her role as homemaker and mother. Mr. Chourré liked teaching in the print shop of Tamalpais High School. They were a happy couple. Their home was unpretentious and immaculate. Windows shone, curtains were crisp, chairs were comfortable, but there was no particular color scheme. Mrs. Chourré thought women who went in for "interior decoration" superficial and their families probably uncomfortable. A house should be comfortable for the people who lived in it. Even Dick's dog, Chuck, had his own ottoman in the living room. At the Chourrés' even the dog was comfortable. I thought sadly of Mother closing the blinds so our furniture would not fade and not allowing me to sit on the bed because I might wrinkle the spread and break down the edge of the mattress. Jane and Marianne shared an L-shaped bedroom furnished with two cots and a dressing table made of orange crates. They sat on their cots anytime they felt like it.

And the food! After the quantity cooking at Stebbins, every meal was a treat, for Mrs.

Chourré was an exquisite cook whose kitchen habits fascinated me. As she cooked, she kept a pan of soapy water in the sink. As soon as she used a utensil, she washed it. When Thanksgiving dinner for twelve was on the table, there wasn't one dirty dish in the kitchen.

The Chourrés were a family who found pleasure in small things: the begonias Mr. Chourré grew in a lath-house, the richness of their compost heap, a game of Scrabble, a casserole dish they called "Smells to Heaven." Jane was making an afghan out of squares of bright scraps of yarn woven on a small loom. Her whole family helped out. Mr. Chourré wove a yellow square on which Jane embroidered POP in turquoise yarn. It seemed to me that everything the Chourrés did had a touch of originality about it. Mrs. Chourré kept on the mantelpiece a small box of misspellings of the family name that she clipped from envelopes that came to the house. One of the misspellings was "Chowsie." Jane and I often referred to her family as the Chowsies.

After Thanksgiving, Clarence began to meet me at the library in the evening and to walk me back to Stebbins. Women were warned against walking alone on the campus at night. Once we went by way of the Greek Theater, where we ran out on the stage and pretended to lead a yell at a football rally:

> "Oski wow-wow!
> Iskey! Wee-wee!
> Holy—Mucky—Eye!
> Holy—Berkeley—Eye!
> California!
> Wow!"

We were startled when applause came out of the dark.

Back at Stebbins, we lingered just long enough on the steps so no one could accuse us of lingering. Clarence walked a lot that year because he then walked back across the campus to his boardinghouse, a Victorian house run by a woman the men called Skipper, where he shared a room with a premed student, Ken. Many years later their room was immortalized in the film *The Graduate,* when it became Dustin Hoffman's college room.

Not that I saw much of that room. Women were strictly forbidden in men's rooms, and vice versa. I was there only once, when Clarence had a bad case of flu and did not go to Cowell Hospital because the staff might keep him too long, and he would lose his job. Ken telephoned me and said Clarence would like to see me. Risking my reputation, I went. Chaperoned by Ken, but feeling guilty, I stood in the doorway to avoid germs and talked to a very pale, bedridden Clarence, who looked even thinner than usual. After a few minutes, I hurried back across the campus, half expecting the dean to pop out from behind a bush.

Mother would have been horrified. She had cautioned me never, never to go to a man's room, and she was already suspicious of Clarence, whom I frequently mentioned in letters because I knew Mother was intensely interested in my social life, far more than in my studies. Once she asked if Clarence had an Irish grandfather. This seemed an odd question. I was too naïve to see what Mother was getting at, so I asked Clarence about his ancestor. Yes, he had had an Irish grandfather but had never seen him. Well! This must mean Clarence was a Catholic, Mother wrote, and she told me I would be wise to drop him at once.

Mother's judgment seemed questionable to me. Yes, Clarence was a Catholic. What difference did it make? We enjoyed each other's company, that was all. Nothing serious, I assured Mother. I planned to finish college, go to library school, and work for at least a year before I married anyone. That was what she advised, and for once we agreed.

This did not satisfy Mother. Clarence and I might get serious, and that would never do. No one on either side of my family had ever married a Catholic. I mentioned Clarence less often in my letters but continued to see him. When spring came, we went for long Sunday afternoon walks in the Berkeley Hills, where acacia bloomed, eucalyptus trees gave off their pungent fragrance, and through the trees we caught glimpses of the bay sparkling in the sun and dotted with sailboats. Gradually I saw less of other men and more of Clarence.

My Intellectual Life

Living at Stebbins Hall and dating were educational, but there was more to life at Cal. Much, much more. That first week of classes I started off with a light heart, eager anticipation, and a new binder filled with pale green paper, which was supposed to be easy on the eyes. The Campanile measured our days and lightened our steps. I was always amused when it played "Mighty Lak' a Rose," the bells bonging out, "Sweetest little fellow . . . "

It was a week of surprises, beginning with class size. Except for a small class in German, which I was taking because it was required for library school, and English 117J, Shakespeare for English majors, which was given in sections limited to forty students, classes seemed enormous after the small classes at Chaffey. English 125C, The Novel, had several hundred students, and so did Psychology 170, Developmental Psychology. Philosophy 5A filled what was called Wheeler Aud, which must have held almost a thousand students.

Professors began to lecture, and, with fountain pen, I began to take notes, a new experience for me, although a high school English teacher had warned her class, "When you go to college you will have to take notes," and for half an hour had read while her class tried to distill the essence of her words. Essence-distilling was more difficult at Cal. I thought of the knitting we had done in class at Chaffey. Why hadn't we been taking notes?

Students were as impersonal as any attending a lecture in a civic auditorium, with one exception. Because I *looked* like someone who could take good notes, attractive men would sometimes sit beside me and strike up a conversation, not because they were interested in me, I soon discovered, but because they wanted to borrow my notes, which I refused to lend, no matter how charming the borrower might be. I suspected good-looking note-borrowers were so unscrupulous they might not bother to return my notes.

Miriam, who was majoring in economics, and I worked out an unusual study schedule, or rather, she worked it out and I went along with it because it suited us. At eight o'clock every evening, Miriam drank a large glass of water so she would have to get up at four in the morning. She then slept soundly. When I came in from the library, I was careful not to wake her while I studied for an hour or so at my desk before I went to bed. Sometimes I would wake up early, usually when the steam radiator began to clank, and see Miriam studying in the circle of light from her gooseneck lamp. She was wearing a warm bathrobe, but her feet in thin leather travel slippers were blue with cold. Although she may have felt cold feet helped her stay awake, I wished I could afford to buy her a pair of warm, woolly slippers. If she saw that I was awake, she often said, "Why am I studying this *stuff*?" which meant she was working on statistics. If she was not at her desk, she was in the bathroom whispering her Latin vocabulary. She could be sure of an A in Latin, which made her scholarship more secure.

Students' worries over grades still puzzled me. Except for that D in Botany, which had been changed to a B+, I had never really worried about grades. If a subject interested me, I earned an A; if it did not, I plodded through to fulfill requirements and earned a B. After all, like Mother, I had my pride. It had not occurred to me that all the students at Cal were equally good, even better, or they wouldn't be there.

Now I heard worried conversations about professors who "graded on the curve," which seemed to have different meanings for different professors but appeared to mean that for every A a D should be given, the number of B's should equal the number of C's. This seemed unjust to me. Did professors never find themselves with a class of brilliant students, all of whom deserved A's? Apparently not. Some students were labeled by others as "D.A.R.s," which stood for "Damned Average Raisers."

I still was not worried about grades, and so one afternoon when I had free time I climbed the stairs to the School of Librarianship to inquire about courses that might be useful to a children's librarian. The secretary eyed me with such a haughty look that I lost my confidence and felt exactly what I was, an immature student in bobby socks.

"The school offers little in children's work," she said and added, "Are you an A student?" in a tone that implied she was sure I wasn't.

"Well—no," I admitted. "So far A's and B's."

She said, "I'm sorry," which she obviously

wasn't. "The students in the School of Librarianship are almost entirely A students." She turned her attention to the work on her desk.

Abashed in my bobby socks, I left. As I descended the stairs I felt defeated and then angry. How dare this woman treat a student, any student, with such arrogance? My wavering confidence stiffened. I was sure I had something to offer, and I was not at all sure straight A's would have anything to do with it. I returned to my room, wrote to the University of Washington for a catalog of their courses in librarianship, and got on with my studies.

The course that I looked forward to three times a week was The Novel, taught by Professor Benjamin Lehman, who had once been married to the actress Judith Anderson, which impressed his students. At first I was dubious about Professor Lehman because he began by speaking out against students who worked their way through college. In Europe, he said, students devoted all their time to their studies. I thought of the men who had started the student cooperatives at Cal. They had been so determined to go to the university that they had worked in the fields all summer and were paid in produce, which kept them going through the first year while they organized the cooperatives and attended classes. Although

Professor Lehman's remarks seemed cruel to me, his course came to mean more to me than any other course I have ever taken.

Professor Lehman was a short, slightly stooped man who entered the classroom at the last minute, faced the class from behind the lectern, and delivered fascinating lectures on novels, beginning with *Pamela,* the first of fourteen or fifteen novels we read that year. At the end of the lecture he turned and walked straight out the door. One sentence that he repeated has stayed with me all my life, and I often think of it as I write: "The proper subject of the novel is universal human experience." A phrase that has also stayed with me is "the minutiae of life," those details that give reality to fiction. It is a long leap from *Peregrine Pickle, Tristram Shandy, The Mysteries of Udolpho,* and all the other novels we studied that year to the books I was to write about Henry, Ramona, and Leigh Botts, but I know, if others may not, that the influence of Professor Lehman is there. I was so pressured, however, that I studied *Tom Jones* without realizing it was a funny story, and I was not the only one.

For English 117I, Shakespeare, I have checked in my text eight plays that we read that semester. English 117J, "designed primarily for juniors whose major subject is English," dealt with nine more plays, as well as Shakespeare's development as a dramatist and the relationship of his work to the Elizabethan theater and to contemporary thought and literature. Both courses were taught by Professor Guy Montgomery, a little man who wore a beard like that on the well-known bust of Shakespeare. He gave more life to the works of Shakespeare than my former teachers. I could compare because I had already studied *Macbeth* in high school and junior college. I am probably the only student in the United States to major in English without studying *Hamlet*. With the dread Comprehensive looming, I read but never actually studied it.

Philosophy 5A and 5B were taught by Professor Pepper, who pronounced *idea* as if it had an *r* on the end and said he would automatically fail anyone who wrote examinations in green ink. We read Lucretius and Plato the first semester and Berkeley, Tawney, Hume, and Dewey the second semester. The large class was divided into discussion groups that met once a week. In one of these groups I wrote down a discussion in my section. I wish I had kept it because it revealed that no one, student or section leader, had any idea what he was talking about.

In choosing my German course I took the advice of Stebbins girls: Never study a foreign language from someone with a name in the same language because the course will be much more difficult. I chose to take the course from a Mr. Corrigan, who in spite of his Irish name turned out to be a blue-eyed blond. I plodded along with a class of mostly men who were planning to be engineers or medical students.

The subject matter of Developmental Psychology was interesting, but the professor was not. He had tan hair, wore a tan suit and tan tie, and spoke in a monotone that I thought of as a tan voice. I suspect he did not enjoy teaching undergraduates and was eager to get back to his graduate students, a common failing of Cal professors.

Midterm examinations were enlightening. On the way to class we stopped at the corner drugstore to buy blue pamphlets in which to write our examinations, which were to be graded by "readers" who were graduate students. Professors, it seemed to me, did not stoop to read examinations, although, to be fair, they probably did read those their readers considered best—or worst.

Stebbins circulated a myth that it was possible to outwit a reader by writing "Second Blue Book" on the front and writing one brilliant last sentence inside. This was supposed to make the reader believe he had lost the first blue book, which would fill him with such guilt that, rather than admit to carelessness, he would give the student an A.

Several days after midterms, the blue books were piled alphabetically on the floor outside classrooms. When I collected mine, I was shocked. Instead of A's and B's, I had sunk to B's and C's. What was wrong? Obviously, I must work harder, and others felt the same way. We no longer sang on our way to the library or played games on the lawn of the Pacific School of Religion.

One of my problems was the tremendous amount of reading in small print required in English courses. The print in the Oxford Standard Edition of Shakespeare was finer than that of the Bible. The print in many novels we read was also fine. German, in those days, was printed in Gothic rather than in Roman type, which was difficult to read with the best of eyes. Once more I broke my vow of never asking my parents for anything and wrote home saying I needed glasses. Once more Mother wrote that I was *not* to wear glasses. I should drop out of school and come home. Why? Probably because she wanted me home and did not want my appearance marred by glasses. So I struggled on, unable to afford glasses and unaware that Cowell Hospital, always sympathetic to student health problems, might have helped.

Second midterms were not much better than the first. And then finals. A saxophone player in the apartment house next door poured sorrow into "Solitude." I sat at my desk and looked out at the limp, dejected underwear dripping in the rain on the clotheslines. Evenings, from time to time and for no reason, male voices would call out, "Pe-e-dro-o-o-o," a sad and lonely sound, a Cal custom whose origins were lost, if not in the mists of time, in the fog of San Francisco.

Tension mounted at Stebbins. Some students stayed up all night to study, or tried to. One girl took a pill to keep awake all night, and at breakfast reported, "It was horrible. I desperately wanted to sleep and couldn't." Another girl, who had been issued one sleeping pill by Cowell Hospital, told us, "I woke up feeling as if I hadn't slept at all."

In those days, before ballpoint pens, we filled our fountain pens, emptied them, and refilled them just to make sure. We self-addressed postcards to enclose in our blue books so readers could send us our grades before official grades came out. Then, as was the Cal custom the first day of finals, the Campanile tolled "An' they're hangin' Danny Deever in the morn'."

Pessimists brought bottles of ink in case their pens ran dry. Sometimes a student without a watch brought a noisy clock that ticked on the nerves of the rest of the class. Mimeographed sheets of questions were passed out. The professor ostentatiously left the room, for Cal operated on the honor system. We read, contemplated, estimated time for each answer, and began to write. I did not have a watch, so I had to rely on my time sense. As we wrote, someone's pen was sure to leak and a profane word was whispered. In every exam I have ever taken, someone, almost always a man, arose from his chair long before the Campanile struck the hour, dropped his blue book on a table at the front of the room, and walked out, leaving the rest of us to wonder if he was brilliant and found the exam so easy he finished quickly or if he found the exam so difficult it was hopeless.

The honor system seemed to work in all my classes except German. As soon as the instructor left the room, answers were whispered back and forth and, once, announced to the whole class. I gritted my teeth, tried to tune everyone out, and clung to my honor even though I knew I would never excel in German.

At Stebbins we watched the mail for postcards. Most of us were disappointed, although the reader for Psychology 170 added a kind note to my postcard telling me I had written an excellent final but he could not give me an A because I had not done well in the first midterm. He gave me a B. I had a respectable B average, but where were all the A's I was used to?

Cal gave us a month's vacation between semesters, so we did not feel we should be writing papers or studying for finals like Oregon students. Miriam and I washed our windows; I packed my bag, said good-bye to Clarence, and, discouraged, took the train to Portland for my first Christmas at home since I was in high school. I was ashamed. My father had borrowed on his life insurance to pay my nonresident tuition, my mother frequently reminded me of the sacrifices she made for me, and now I was not living up to their expectations. Sleeping in a Pullman car was difficult. I dozed, and at Dunsmuir, in the middle of the night, the train backed and bumped as another engine, facing backward, was added to the rear to help push the train over the mountains. It reminded me of the pushmi-pullyu, an animal with a head at either end in the Dr. Dolittle books I had read and reread as a child.

The next evening the train, late arriving in

Portland, waited on the east side of the Willamette River while a bridge was raised for a ship to pass through. There was nothing to do but watch the Sherwin-Williams sign, a paint can outlined in electric lights pouring paint made of hundreds of electric bulbs over a huge globe of the world. The words COVER THE EARTH lit up, the lights were extinguished, and the pouring of electric paint began again. Hypnotized by the sign, I wanted to sit on the prickly train seat for hours rather than move on into Union Station.

When the ship passed by, the bridge closed and the train crossed the river. My eager parents had arrived early because, as Mother explained, "We like to watch the people." Mother's mother, Grandma Atlee, proper in her old-fashioned hat and gloves, was sitting quietly, waiting.

"Where's Grandpa?" I asked, puzzled. Mother explained that she had not wanted to tell me during finals, but he was in the hospital with what had turned out to be inoperable cancer and Grandma was now living with us. I appreciated her consideration, but the news was a shock. Somehow I had expected my grandparents to live forever.

There was another surprise. Dad had bought a car. He explained that when he lost his job and had to sell his car in 1929, he held back some money that he invested in General Motors stock, which had increased in value until he could afford another Chevrolet, now a necessity because of my grandmother.

On the drive home I inhaled the fragrance of a new car and confessed that I was not doing as well at Cal as I had expected. I knew I could count on understanding from Dad, but I was not so sure about Mother. Here was another surprise. She said gently, "Too bad. You'll do better next time." I hoped I would.

Whenever Dad turned a corner, Grandma whispered, "Oh, Lordy!" Except for a brief time when, over Mother's protests, Grandpa had bought and wildly driven a Model T Ford, Grandma had never ridden in an automobile until she came to live with us. Grandma called me Mable, Mother's name, and referred to Dad as "that gentleman." Our amusement covered sorrow. I had known my grandmother's memory was failing, but I had not expected it to drift so far away.

The next evening, because neither Mother nor I could drive, a friend drove us to St. Vincent's Hospital to see my grandfather while my father stayed with my grandmother. My dear, kindhearted, funny Grandpa, drugged into half-sleep, lay in a narrow bed in a cheerless room. He opened his eyes, said, "Mable," and sank into deep sleep. Could he possibly know how much he meant to me? Memories overwhelmed me: Grandpa holding me on his knee and teaching me arithmetic before I started school; Grandpa's vegetable garden, where I had loved to pick up new potatoes when he turned over the soil; Grandpa's strawberry bed; Grandpa behind the counter of his general merchandise store measuring coffee into the red coffee grinder, cutting slabs of Tillamook cheese with a small guillotine, and weighing out bulk tea and oatmeal; Grandpa letting me help myself to gumdrops and cutting off "remnants" from bolts of fabric so I could make doll clothes; Grandpa joshing with drummers who came by train with heavy trunks to sell bolts of fabric, thread, stockings, corsets, and all the things my grandmother sold on her side of the store. That evening was the last time I saw my grandfather. After that I stayed with my grandmother while Dad drove Mother to the hospital.

In spite of her grief, Mother did not forget my social life. An Anglophile because she had loved her English grandparents so much, she was interested in the Commonwealth Fellows and asked many questions about them before she got down to what was really on her mind. Did I still see Clarence? Yes, I did, but not exclusively. She repeated that I would be wise to drop him. After all, he was Catholic. Why did I no longer mention Jack? I told her, with wry amusement, the story of Jack the Bounder. At first she was shocked that such a man would be a member of the Masonic Club, where she had counted on my meeting nice young men. Then she said with a sigh, "Well, I suppose it was good experience for you." I agreed. From Jack I had learned to trust my instincts.

Claudine's return from Dee for her Christmas vacation was a relief from the sorrow and tension at home. I usually spent afternoons at her house, where we had privacy because Mrs. Klum was often out playing bridge. Claudine, never one to complain, did drop bits of information that I pieced together. Teaching in an isolated sawmill town was an experience she endured rather than enjoyed, even though she liked her first- and second-grade children, a number of them Japanese. She and an uncongenial teacher shared a room in the house of a young married couple who lived outside town. The wife packed their lunches, which every single day consisted of sandwiches made of white bread and bottled sandwich spread of mayonnaise and chopped pickle with no meat, not even bologna. Dessert

161

was always a piece of chocolate cake. Dinners were not much better. Once a week she served wieners and sauerkraut.

The mill town was cold and lonely. Claudine and her roommate corrected papers in the evening and went to bed early. There was nothing else to do. There was no library, not even a bookmobile. The only way out of Dee was to ask the highway patrol for a ride to Hood River, where Claudine could catch a bus to Portland. I could see that she dreaded returning. She was wistful about my life at Cal, and her eighty dollars a month seemed like a fortune to me.

When I had to admit that Stebbins's monthly fee had been raised, my parents were shocked. What I had considered a challenge, they considered a hardship. I insisted I was able to manage, but Dad said, "I can scrape up another six dollars a month." He also scraped up money for a wristwatch for Christmas.

It was a sad vacation. My nervous mother was exhausted from trips to the hospital. My gentle grandmother, confused in her new home, sat in a chair by the dining room window. "She has nothing to do," said Mother, and snipped holes in our sugar-sack dish towels for Grandma to mend, work she enjoyed. Her stitches were as tiny and neat as the stitches in clothes she had made for me when I was in the first grade. The memory of her marriage of over sixty years was gone. She never once mentioned my grandfather, whom she had married at the age of seventeen to escape a stepmother. Now she had only one memory left, a memory of her childhood in Michigan. When friends came to visit, she would sit quietly, apparently interested in the conversation. Then, when there was a pause, she would smile and say with pride, "Father gave the land for the school."

I was not sorry to board the Southern Pacific for Berkeley even though I was confused and worried about my future, the one subject Mother had not cross-examined me on, and with all her troubles, I could not add to them by admitting that Cal's library school would not find my grades acceptable, that after feeling the atmosphere of the place, I did not even want to be admitted. Teaching? No, I did not want to teach. My grammar school days had left me with several bitter memories, but I knew others had memories far more bitter. I did not want to become an unhappy memory to children trapped in a classroom. Children were free to come and go in a library.

I tried but could not imagine a future for myself as the train pulled out of the station and the Sherwin-Williams sign drenched the earth with electric paint, retrieved it, and drenched it again.

Two Vacations

Returning to the cheerful confusion of Stebbins was a relief after the tense, sad days in Portland. Then, on January 17, my grandfather died. Mother wrote that he had tried to climb over the bed railing, fallen, and contracted pneumonia. "It was a blessing," Mother said. "Pneumonia is an old man's friend." Poor Grandpa, so nimble as he climbed up and down a ladder to reach merchandise on the top shelves of his store, which had become the town's center. I couldn't bear to think of this kindhearted eighty-five-year-old man suffering alone on a cold hospital floor.

Grandpa's death was a sad start for a new semester. Mother, worn-out from hospital visits, the care of my grandmother, and the disposal of my grandfather's store and the post office building he owned, did not remember that I no longer received money from him. I missed his monthly five dollars. But I held to my vow of never asking for money, so I shortened more skirts, and Mrs. Cochran paid me to make her a silk dressing gown she could slip into when she had to get up to unlock the front door for girls who had overstayed the two-thirty deadline. (Most, however, bypassed Mrs. Cochran by climbing in the ground-floor windows of accommodating friends.)

With one exception, my second-semester courses were the same as the first. Because I was not giving up on becoming a children's librarian and writing children's books, I decided courses in education might be useful. Unfortunately, Education 101, History of Education, was a prerequisite for any course in elementary education.

History of Education was the sort of class that began with students counting minutes, hoping the professor would be late, for Cal had an unwritten rule that if a professor was ten minutes late, students could leave. This one was always on time. All I remember about the uninteresting, to me, lectures was the professor's several references to Saint Simeon Stylites, who lived on top of a pillar for thirty-six years to call attention to the evils of his time. I do not recall why this uncomfortable saint was mentioned at all.

What I do recall is the paper the entire class was required to write on one subject, "Plato: Teacher and Theorist." This paper had to be twenty-four pages long. Not twenty-three, not twenty-five. Twenty-four. Fortunately, I was fresh from Plato the previous semester, but I resented every word of that paper, every footnote, every *ibid.,* every *op. cit.,* and longed to add one footnote, "I thought of this myself." Footnotes in foreign languages, according to the wisdom of Stebbins, always impressed a reader, but I couldn't work one in on Plato. Someday, *someday,* I vowed, I would write entire books without footnotes.

For some masochistic reason, I felt I should take a course in physical education even though this was not required of juniors. I have no idea why I felt this way because students got plenty of exercise climbing stairs and hurrying up and down hills. I chose Fencing, which surprised and amused athletic Clarence. Nevertheless, épée in hand and protected by a wire-mesh mask and quilted plastron, I lunged, parried, and thrust my way to a surprising B. Touché, Clarence Cleary! The educational residue of this course was a critical attitude toward fencing in movies. Very sloppy, most of it seems to me, but then I did not have to duel my way up and down staircases.

At the end of my junior year, I took the train once more for Portland, where Sherwin-Williams still covered the earth. I was filled with ambition to study for the Comprehensive, that literary doomsday for English majors.

Because Cal's spring semester ended in May and the University of Oregon's in June, Virginia, a high school friend, invited me to come to Eugene to stay at her sorority house and attend a dance. She had rounded up the brother of a boy I had known in high school to escort me. I drove to Eugene with Bob, her fiancé, a young man I had introduced her to several years before.

That weekend in a sorority house was quite different from life at Stebbins. A number of girls were engaged to be married, which seemed the fashionable thing to do in those days when many Oregon parents sent their daughters to college to "catch a husband," an expression I had never heard applied to Cal. The girls were not treated like adults. Immediately after the dance they were expected to return to the sorority house, where the housemother stood at the door. There were no kisses, no lingering goodnights. The girls slept on a sleeping porch in double-decker bunks like those in the Camp Fire Girls' summer camp, and most girls had their own busily ticking alarm clock. On school days the ringing must have been even more annoying than the thumping, whacking steam radiators of Stebbins Hall.

The dining room was attractive and homelike, but conversation was not as lively as that of Stebbins girls, probably because the housemother, unlike Mrs. Cochran, presided. After breakfast we attended a softball game and a beery fraternity picnic. I was glad I was attending Cal.

I had a glimpse of Claudine before her school was out. She had decided she could not face another bleak year in Dee with sandwich-spread sandwiches and chocolate cake, so one Saturday she took a carsick bus trip down the Columbia River Highway to Portland, a ride that did not make most Oregonians carsick because they stopped and got out of their cars to admire every waterfall along the way. Once again Claudine's mother and a friend drove Claudine to a suburb to be interviewed by a school superintendent, who was also the owner of a roadhouse. It was late afternoon, but he and his wife were dressed for work, he in a tuxedo and she in a long evening dress. Claudine was ill at ease and so, apparently, was he. After a few hurried questions, he said, "Take off your coat and walk around the room." He was used to hiring dancers, not teachers. Embarrassed, Claudine did as she was told, and she was hired. She returned to Dee to finish the remaining days of her bleak school year.

I tried to do some reading that might be useful in taking the Comprehensive, but somehow I had trouble concentrating. My mind wandered from Milton to Clarence and to Berkeley, where I could in my "right hand lead with thee, the mountain nymph, sweet Liberty," the only lines from Milton that I could remember, and ones that I had learned in high school.

Sweet Liberty was scarce in Portland that summer. While Mother shopped or went to the library, I stayed with my grandmother and knit a red dress with yarn I had been able to buy when Miriam admired the pink silk dress I had knit at Chaffey so much that she asked to buy it. I also sewed, making a dress for myself and a dress for Mother. I helped can, or "put up," tomatoes, peaches, and string beans in the steamy kitchen, an annual chore.

I was lonely and missed Claudine. When her semester ended in Dee, she decided to take her savings from eighty dollars a month and attend summer session at the University of Washington. This surprised me. While I had been traveling up and down the coast, Claudine had stayed close to home.

While Claudine was gone, Olive Miles, a neighboring school friend, and I stayed with Grandma for a week while my parents went to the beach so Mother could rest. I shopped and cooked while Olive took care of Grandma, helping her dress, guiding her to the bathroom, helping her to bed. We both listened politely whenever Grandma told us, "Father gave the land for the school."

With Claudine gone so long and other friends working, the summer seemed endless. I missed the leisurely days at Puddin', and I felt guilty because I could not bring myself to study Milton.

Mother was concerned. "Why don't you write?" she suggested.

My mind was a blank, but I did write. I wrote letters to Clarence, who was working full-time in Bedding and Linen during the summer. This was not what Mother had in mind.

Clarence wrote that he wanted to telephone me. What would be a good time? A long-distance call— I had never talked long-distance. I wrote that he should call me on Friday evening because that was the time my parents left to do the week's marketing while I stayed with my grandmother.

At dinner that evening, because I was so excited, I foolishly remarked that Clarence was going to telephone me about seven-thirty.

Mother went rigid with disapproval. "We don't have to shop this evening," she informed me.

I was bewildered. "But you always go to market on Friday night."

"We are not going to be driven out of our own house," she said.

I couldn't believe what I was hearing. When Jane had expected a long-distance call from a man, the entire Chourré family climbed into their car and went for a ride so she could have privacy.

The minutes ticked by on my grandfather's clock on the mantel as we all sat silent, tense. The telephone rang and I answered, glad to hear Clarence's gentle voice but furious because Mother and Dad were listening to every word I said. We talked briefly before I burst into tears, tears because he was so far away, tears because I was not allowed a few minutes of privacy. The call was short. I did not want to waste Clarence's money on tears.

Afterward I went to my room, threw myself on my bed, and wept in anger. There was silence in the living room until Dad came in, sat down on the bed, patted my back, tried to comfort me, and said he was sorry. I did not see Mother until the next morning. Never one to apologize or admit she had done anything wrong, she was tight-lipped and our conversation was stiff.

Claudine's return from the University of Washington was a relief. I could go to her house in the afternoon. She reported that she had taken all the music she could crowd in and had excelled in every course except one. For some reason as illogical as my taking fencing, Claudine, who could play anything she heard on the piano, had taken a course in the clarinet. Perhaps she was influenced by Benny Goodman, for this was the beginning of the Swing Era. She said all she could get out of the clarinet was a squawk. I reminded her of the time she had tried to give me piano lessons. As I struggled, she said, "Just *play* it." My playing made her so impatient we finally gave up. We found this episode funny, and whenever we faced difficulty, told each other to "just *play* it."

I soon had an opportunity to try to just play it. One afternoon when a letter from Clarence slid through the mail slot, I sat down in the living room to read it. Mother, sitting on the davenport, looked up from her book to watch me. When I had finished the letter and returned it to its envelope, she asked with a sprightly smile, artificially sprightly I knew, "Well, what does he say?"

"Oh, nothing much," I answered, and added in an attempt at conversation, "His roommate wants to move into an apartment next semester and wants him to go along."

Mother dropped her book and sat up straight. "You are *not* to go to that apartment," she informed me.

I was astonished. Obviously, I had done a poor job of just "playing it." "I wasn't planning to," I said quite truthfully because such an idea had not entered my head. The apartment, I guessed, would be on the south side of the campus in a run-down Victorian house with peeling paint.

"Just see that you don't," said Mother. "No nice girl goes to a man's apartment."

I considered this remark. Once Wilfrid and Campbell had invited Miriam and me for dinner in the attractive apartment they shared on the north side of the campus, an area that had been destroyed by fire in the 1920s and rebuilt with modern homes and apartment buildings. The table was tastefully decorated with a stack of cans of Campbell soup in honor of Campbell. Perhaps it was his birthday. The evening was innocent, and Miriam and I remained as nice as when we had accepted the invitation. Probably we left soon after dinner because Miriam went to bed so early.

After learning of the apartment, Mother grew more intense. At dinner, with her mouth set in a straight line that gave the meal a trial-like atmosphere so familiar from high school days, she informed Dad that Clarence was moving into an apartment. No wrath was brought down upon my head. Dad accepted the news calmly. Later, he took me aside and said quietly, "It's a good idea to be careful about going to a man's apartment."

"Of course," I said, noting that he didn't say I should not go. He just said I should be careful. Dad trusted me and felt I was sensible enough to make my own decisions.

Finally the day came for me to leave. On the way to Union Station, with Grandma in her hat and gloves saying, "Lordy!" every time we turned a corner, Mother said, "Under the circumstances, most parents wouldn't let you go back to college."

I didn't answer. All I wanted to do was get on that train and escape, even if it meant facing the Comprehensive.

Clarence and the Comprehensive

The bells of the Campanile, and even the smell of catsup, lifted my spirits when I returned to Cal. Red roses from Clarence delivered by a florist, the wildest extravagance, lifted them even more. I kept the roses until their petals faded to dull purple and finally dropped softly to my desk. Clarence invited me to dinner at his apartment, and of course I went. Steak, boiled potatoes, and canned corn. The place was as dreary as I had imagined, with one room, a kitchen not much larger than a closet, and a bath. The one decorative touch was a sock filled with tennis balls suspended from the ceiling light fixture. Clarence and Ken used it for a punching bag.

The immediate problem at Stebbins was our choice of courses. We thumbed our General Catalogues, asked one another to give us the lowdown on professors of courses we were considering. Several girls said, "Why did I ever choose *this* major?" and changed majors, letting themselves in for a heavy schedule if they were to graduate in May.

From the list of courses "designed primarily for seniors whose major subject is English" I chose Chaucer. Milton lurked on the list, but since Chaucer was a one-semester course, I felt I could postpone Milton for a few months. Other English majors said I shouldn't miss The Age of Johnson, a great course. I followed their advice. I also chose Advanced French Grammar, not because I thirsted for more irregular verbs, but because the University of Washington School of Librarianship required more units of French than I had on my record. Having endured History of Education, I was now entitled to enroll in Elementary Education, which Jane was also taking. I still needed three more units. I longed for a course in household arts but did not have the prerequisites. I had, I discovered, prerequisites for very little. I finally settled on Anthropology 105, The American Indian, as the most possible course open to me. Besides, I reminded myself, all knowledge is useful to librarians.

Elementary Education offered unexpected entertainment, not because of the professor, an interesting, kindly man understanding of both children and teachers, but because of a student, an older woman, an experienced teacher who, like other out-of-state teachers, was working toward a California credential because California salaries were higher than those of other states. She arrived at the morning class with liquor on her breath and interesting comments to make. The project method of teaching was in fashion at that time. Choose a project such as American Indians that interests children, and they will be so eager to learn they will read, and so eager to build a tepee they will learn arithmetic. The experienced teacher never hesitated to speak out. "What are we supposed to do with all this garbage if they ever finish their tepee?" she once asked. I could picture the tepee made of sticks covered with brown paper or old sheets. How would the children make it stand up? Another memorable remark was "We would be too tired to go dancing after a day with all that junk." Jane and I found this course especially interesting for the wrong reason.

Advanced French Grammar was something to dread, for I had not studied French grammar for two years. The small class was taught by Mme Habis-Reutinger. The students were all girls, most of them members of sororities, many of them with excellent accents from having studied French in private schools. A couple actually had been to France. The class, for me, was a nightmare of idioms and elaborate grammatical constructions. I dreaded being called on to read aloud. Eventually I was. In a small voice I stumbled along as best I could, and when I finished, Madame smiled and said, "Oh, dat is so sweet." A kind woman, she did not call on me to read aloud again.

Anthropology 105. After a class in a building at the bottom of the campus, I raced uphill to a small building at the top, pausing for a few words with Clarence, who was heading downhill. I usually arrived after all the seats had been taken, sat on a cold steam radiator, and left the class with a corrugated bottom. The course was taught by a lecturer, Alfred Métraux, a famous anthropologist, although I did not realize it at the time. As I recall, he taught at Cal only a semester or two, and I was lucky to have chosen his course, for he was a fascinating man in spite of a heavy French accent. He skipped quickly over North

America and lectured on South America, where he had actually lived with the tribes mentioned in our textbook, a book he seemed to regard as a nuisance. I remember his vivid account of a ship dropping him off at Tierra del Fuego, the southernmost tip of South America, a raw and windy place where the native inhabitants had not discovered that their animal skins would be warmer if they wore the fur inside. With a rueful laugh, Mr. Métraux told how cold he had been and how he was afraid the ship would forget to pick him up, leaving him stranded in that bleak place forever.

Alfred Métraux did not often laugh and obviously did not enjoy teaching. He was particularly irritated by one member of the class, a graduate student in anthropology, a neat, earnest, precise woman who always sat in the middle of the front row. Whenever Mr. Métraux mentioned in his French accent an unfamiliar term or tribal name, she raised her hand and said, "Excuse me. How do you spell that?" Through gritted teeth he spelled it. When mid-terms came, he gave her a C, shocking all the graduate students, who could not get C's and remain graduate students. I have often wondered what her final grade was and if Mr. Métraux left her career in shards as he fled Cal for jungles.

Chaucer, the smallest class I had at Cal, was given in sections of twenty students. I was fortunate in choosing Professor Arthur Brodeur, who was recommended by Stebbins girls. He was a handsome, gentlemanly man with white hair who read from *The Canterbury Tales* and *The Book of the Duchess* in a rich and musical voice. Professor Brodeur endeared himself to me by his punctuality in keeping office hours and because he stood when I entered. No other professor had shown me such courtesy. He patiently discussed possible subjects for a paper I was to write, and when I left his office, he again rose to his feet.

Next to The Novel, my favorite course at Cal was The Age of Johnson, taught by Assistant Professor Bertrand Bronson. Students referred to the course as The Age of Bronson. The text was the Oxford edition of Boswell's *Life of Johnson* in very fine print. Instead of our reading straight through, Professor Bronson divided the book, assigning reading according to subject, which made the eighteenth century extraordinarily vivid. Several years later I happened to meet Mrs. Bronson and told her how much pleasure her husband's course had given me. She smiled and said, "I'll tell him. He often wonders." And I had thought insecurity was an affliction of students, not professors.

While I divided my time among Clarence, American Indians, eighteenth-century England, and solving problems in pupil behavior in Elementary Education, Miriam continued to study with cold, blue feet and was rewarded. One day she took a rich-looking envelope from our mailbox, and when she opened it, she found she had been elected to Phi Beta Kappa. And in her junior year! The motivated girls of Stebbins Hall, who had the highest grade point average of any students on campus, were proud of her. She borrowed a Phi Beta Kappa key and went off to the initiation with the best wishes of all of us. I felt that anyone who could get out of bed at four o'clock every morning deserved to be honored.

Another Christmas vacation. All I remember about it is snow in Portland, Mother's exhaustion in caring for my grandmother, and her disapproval of Clarence. Dad did not comment on Clarence. I assumed his feelings were neutral. When I returned to Stebbins, Miriam told me she was moving out to share a room with her sister, who had enrolled at Cal. This was a shock, for Miriam and I had lived peacefully with our unusual study schedule and had enjoyed good times together. She, too, was in emotional turmoil. Wilfrid wanted to marry her. She wanted to finish college. The terms of his Fellowship required that he return to England at the end of the semester. Finally, after much anguish, she decided to give up her senior year, marry during the summer, and finish college in England. I missed her.

My next roommate was a beautiful girl, a French major with a broken heart, who seemed to do very little studying. She said she had a photographic memory, which made French easy for her. I liked her and feel I should somehow have been a better friend to her, but like many seniors, I was in too much of an emotional snarl. I often found her weeping over a bundle of letters and some dry, crumbling roses. Late in the evening she sat cross-legged on her bed, a French book on her knees, mentally photographing vocabulary while she put her hair up in thirty-two pin curls.

Early in the second semester I sent off my application, along with my hopes, to the School of Librarianship at the University of Washington. I was disheartened because I was not distinguishing myself at Cal, although today, as I look at my transcript, I can see that at that time I had a respectable B average, higher if all my Chaffey A's were included.

Clarence, in the meantime, had completed his required units midyear, or, as we said, he was a member of the class of 1937½. Because he had been entirely self-supporting during some grim Depression years, he had spent six years in college. Now he said he was tired of studying, of not having enough money, and so, along with many other students, he took civil service examinations. In those days government jobs were coveted because they offered security, and the hope of many students was to become a P-1, Junior Professional Assistant. Bedding and Linen was not Clarence's life ambition, and at that point he was no longer sure what was.

One damp evening after an Assembly Dance where Clarence had sung into my ear "our" songs, "Does Your Heart Beat for Me?" and "You're the One Rose That's Left in My Heart," we walked up the hill past Stebbins to sit on a sheltered wall overlooking Strawberry Creek. The pressures of Cal and of barely having enough money had ground me down to the point where I did not expect to be accepted by the University of Washington. What next? Back to Portland and Mother's relentless supervision? I felt hopeless.

Clarence took me in his arms and said that when he found a job, we could do something about it. We could get married. In those Depression days we had not discussed marriage or even love, although I might have guessed he loved me because he sang so tenderly in his beautiful tenor voice while we danced. I had not allowed myself to think of love and had always thought of marriage as something far in the future. Now, suddenly, I knew I loved and wanted to marry him. We sat in the cold and dark with rain drizzling down and the creek gurgling below us and talked a long time. I was still determined to become self-supporting and to work a year before marriage. He agreed this was probably a wise decision on my part. I also said I would not join the Catholic Church, that I felt my heritage was as valuable to me as his was to him, and the religious education of children would be his responsibility. He said that was all right with him, that he knew I was not cut out to be a Catholic. When he finally said good night under Stebbins's porch light, we lingered longer than Stebbins's propriety considered appropriate.

With Clarence on my mind, I still could not face Milton. The second semester I enrolled in The Age of Swift and Pope, taught by a young man considered a rising star in the English Department. He spoke in a high voice, waved a cigarette in a long holder, and talked about Inglish poy-tree. I stayed in the course long enough to discover that Alexander Pope had written "Hope springs eternal in the human breast" and "A little learning is a dangerous thing," lines that I had assumed belonged to Shakespeare. I counted up my units and discovered I would have enough to graduate without Swift and Pope and the waving cigarette holder. I would have more time to study for the Comprehensive. I could even read Milton.

One spring evening, with Milton in hand, I walked up the hill to sit with the little girl in the house with the spiral staircase. I read to her from *Winnie-the-Pooh* and was settled in a comfortable chair, a rare treat for a student, and there I made the biggest mistake of my life. I put Milton aside and wrote a letter to Mother and Dad telling them Clarence and I planned to marry after I had gone to library school and had worked a year.

Although I should have been prepared for Mother's answer, which came by return mail, I was not. She wrote a brief, angry letter telling me they would give me their answer in a week and to remember I had *promised* I would never marry Clarence. I had done no such thing. I had said, early in our acquaintance, that I had no intention of marrying him, and at that time I didn't. After a dismal week a letter arrived telling me that by marrying Clarence I would be disloyal to my family and to my religion. My parents would not give me their approval. Mother, house-bound with the care of my grandmother, had nothing to do but brood and write letters I dreaded opening.

Pressures weighed more heavily on me. I could scarcely stay awake after lunch. Jane, always understanding, suggested I take a nap in her room so she could wake me in time for my two o'clock class. While calm, organized Jane studied quietly at her desk, I fell into a deep sleep of exhaustion until she woke me, and I went off to The Age of Elizabeth, which I had chosen to follow last semester's The Age of Johnson and allowed me, filled with guilt, to avoid Milton. Elizabethan love lyrics were preferable, but I did skip one assignment, the only assignment I ever skipped, Richard Hooker's *Laws of Ecclesiastical Polity*. I still feel that I should read it, but I know I won't.

Then one spring day I found in our mailbox a letter from the University of Washington. I had been accepted by the School of Librarianship. My Wordsworthian heart leaped again. I dashed off a note to my parents and waited for Clarence to call from Bedding and Linen.

By now all English majors were feeling tired and overwrought. Jane invited me to Mill Valley for spring vacation so we could study for the Comprehensive together. Perhaps we did, a little. Mrs. Chourré, aware of the monotony of dorm food, prepared us a lunch of waffles with fresh strawberries and whipped cream. I recall going for a walk with Jane and climbing a hill covered with wildflowers. We lay in a field of California poppies and lupine that had the fragrance of grape bubble gum and let the sun drain away our tensions. Wildflowers, sunshine, quiet, and the company of a dear friend—it was a lovely afternoon far from the pressures of Cal and of my family.

The Chourrés invited Clarence to come to Mill Valley for Easter dinner. They made him welcome, obviously approved of him, and smiled upon us. There was laughter at the dinner table, and the family enjoyed one another's company. If only my family could be like this, I thought.

The memory of the Chourrés and of serene Mill Valley with its lupine and redwood trees helped sustain me on the trip back to Berkeley and the dread Comprehensive, the first half of which I feared most of all. Chaucer, Shakespeare, and Milton. Everyone said these were the most important writers, and I had eluded Milton as if he were chasing me with a knife. A graduate student called Stebbins's English majors to a meeting in the living room and offered to coach us. None of us could afford his services.

We all bought A *History of English Literature,* by Emile Legouis and Louis Cazamian, translated from the French, which was considered the definitive text. Couldn't the English write their own history? I wondered as I opened it to the section on Milton. My thoughts tumbled, words seemed to make no sense, I could not concentrate. I could only sit at my desk and stare at Stebbins's underwear flapping in the breeze on the garage roofs. When the man next door poured sorrow into "Solitude" on his saxophone, I put my head down on my desk. I dreaded the exam, I dreaded Sherwin-Williams covering the earth, I dreaded Mother bearing down on me with her disapproval of Clarence, whom she had never met.

Then Mrs. Cochran, understanding of all the girls' problems, told me that Stebbins was going to rent rooms to women attending summer school and would need a chambermaid. I snatched the opportunity. Mother had little enthusiasm for my doing menial work, but since I would be doing it in California, where no one in Oregon would see me, she admitted the money would help toward my nonresident tuition in Seattle. She gave the neighbors the impression I was to be a receptionist.

At breakfast the morning of the Comprehensive, we English majors, hollow-eyed, silent, and unsmiling, gathered sympathetic looks from others, as if we were about to have major surgery from which we might not recover. We then collected our freshly filled fountain pens and our blue books. On the way out, I saw a letter from Mother in our mailbox. I left it there.

In the chemistry building, scene of our ordeal, mimeographed questions were passed out. The major question was something like "Discuss the influence of history on English literature." Most English majors had studied history as a minor, but I had not taken history in college and had skimmed lightly over it when it was brought up in English classes. Silly me. A number of students read the questions and left the room, but I tried to thaw my numb brain and plunged in, spreading my knowledge thin.

The second question was about sonnet sequences. I could think of many sonnets but not in sequence. There was Shakespeare, and there was Elizabeth Barrett Browning, but who else? Could I manage to work in the influence of Petrarch? I couldn't keep my thoughts focused. They drifted to the dreaded letter waiting in the mailbox, to Clarence, to anything but sonnet sequences. I felt as if the Campanile, with each passing hour, was knelling disaster. Nevertheless I wrote something, I can't imagine what.

The Stebbins English majors, relieved, exhausted, and surprised that the sun was still shining, compared notes on our way back to the dormitory. Jane taped a sign on her door: "An English major knits up the raveled sleave of care." In room 228 I read Mother's anti-Clarence letter and fell asleep.

In addition to the second half of the Comprehensive, I still had one more exam to take, Advanced French Grammar. I felt exhausted, confused, and incapable of remembering a single idiom. The night before the French exam, Clarence came to Stebbins to try to rescue me. We sat in the living room while he drilled me on grammar and idioms, and I tried to cram into my head a semester's work, desperate to make it stick until I had taken the exam the next day. When Clarence left, I felt as if he were taking my crammed knowledge with him.

Somehow I got through the final and, when it was over, exhaled what little I had learned about Advanced French Grammar. On the postcard I had enclosed in my blue book, Madame wrote: "Mademoiselle, vous n'avez pas étudié." She kindly let me escape with a C, probably because I was a senior.

Then came the day when those of us who had taken the first half of the Comprehensive could telephone the English office to ask for our grades. When I gave my name, the secretary said, "E–."

"What?" I asked, aghast. I had never heard of such a grade.

"A, B, C, D, E–," she said. For a moment I thought she might go on down the alphabet to an even stranger grade, possibly K–.

"Oh" was all I could say, and I hung up and fled to Jane's room to confess and seek comfort. She was as appalled as I and, never having heard of an E–, was sure I had misunderstood. She offered to call the English office and inquire.

"Didn't I give out that grade?" asked the secretary. Jane explained that I couldn't believe it. The secretary confirmed that my grade was indeed an E–, but she did say the Comprehensive would be given again during summer session and I could try it again.

Jane tried to comfort me, pointing out that we still had the second half of the Comprehensive ahead of us, and the two grades would be averaged, so there was still hope. But how, I wondered, did Cal average an E–? I felt like a failure, a guilty failure. My parents' hopes were on my shoulders. I broke the news to them and found Mother sympathetic. She said it was a good thing I was staying in Berkeley for the summer so I could repeat the exam. I knew I was too exhausted to take the exam again, so my only hope lay in The Novel, the subject I had chosen for the second half of the examination.

The day came; I climbed the steps of Wheeler Hall on heavy feet and waited for the questions. There was only one, a statement rather than a question: Discuss the Novel. For three hours I discussed the Novel and emerged exhausted as the Campanile began to play a merry tune. This time when I called the English office, I learned that my grade was a B, which wiped out the disgraceful E– and gave me a D as a final grade. I would graduate. I hoped Cal wouldn't squeal to the University of Washington.

Dad drove to Berkeley alone to attend my graduation. Mother felt she could not entrust the care of her mother to anyone else. The notebook in which he kept a record of his expenses shows that he drove to California inland and returned by the coastal route, thus making the most of his trip. Although he had never spoken one word of complaint about my grandmother living with us, he did not send my mother so much as a postcard during his two weeks of freedom. He and Clarence were friendly when I introduced them, and we enjoyed dinner together. We were more comfortable without Mother.

Graduation in the Memorial Stadium. More than two thousand of the Class of '38 in our caps and gowns lined up behind the professors in their colorful regalia, leaders made sure we were in the right order, and when the time came for us to receive our diplomas, Robert Gordon Sproul, president of the university, handed mine to me and said, "Congratulations *to* you." I was free. The whole thing was so well organized that we each received the right diploma. Clarence refused to take time off from Bedding and Linen, where he was paid by the hour, to attend commencement. I picked up his diploma for him at Cal Hall.

Graduation night. An orchid arrived from Clarence, followed by Clarence himself in Ken's tuxedo with the bow tie untied because Clarence did not know how to tie it. Dad let us take his car, and after stopping at a gas station for an attendant to tie the dangling tie, we were off across the Bay Bridge for a night on the town. Dinner at the Fairmont, dancing at the Palace, more dancing at the Mark Hopkins, where we went to meet friends and made the mistake of sitting down. A waiter handed Clarence a bill for four dollars. What for? "Cover charge, sir," said the waiter. Four dollars just to sit down—we had never heard of such a thing. Fortunately, Clarence had four dollars left as well as twenty-five cents for the bridge toll.

The next day, after a lunch of crab Louis, a meal Dad remembered for years, we took him on a tour of San Francisco. It was a day we all enjoyed. I was happy to see the two get along and sorry to say good-bye to my father the following morning.

Like Cinderella after the ball, I turned into a chambermaid. I often wonder why I remember Cal with such affection.

The Campanile

Miriam, my roommate at Stebbins Hall

Jane on the steps of Doe Library at Cal

Clarence in 1938, wearing the same tie he was wearing when we met (He still has it.)

Clarence keeps his eye on the ball after work in Bedding and Linen.

En garde at Cal

My Cal yearbook picture, class of '38

I escape from Cal.

A happy afternoon in Golden Gate Park with Dad and with Clarence's orchid on my shoulder

Grandma Atlee after she came to live with us

Grandpa Atlee, Uncle Henry, Cousin Zed

PART TWO

Children,
Customers,
Soldiers

Library School

After my narrow escape from Cal, the physical work of a chambermaid was a relief. I moved to a first-floor room next to Mrs. Cochran and, when she was out, answered the door and showed rooms, thus keeping Mother partially honest. I made beds, cleaned bathrooms, ran the vacuum cleaner, counted laundry. Fortunately, not all the forty-one rooms were rented.

To earn my meals I worked an hour before dinner in a men's boardinghouse across the street, where I had various duties: setting the table, making salad, cutting two colors of Jell-O into cubes and heaping them into sherbet dishes so they would look like more dessert than they actually were, ironing shirts for the landlady's sons.

She ran a tight boardinghouse and once reprimanded a summer student from Stanford for asking for butter when he already had jam for his toast, a scene that reminded me of Oliver Twist asking for more gruel. Jamless or butterless, I was happy to be self-supporting, standing on my own two feet for the summer.

Soon after I started my humble chores, Clarence was offered a position by the new Department of Employment in Sacramento. Saturdays he came to Berkeley by train, staying at Skipper's boardinghouse, and we went to a movie in the evening. On Sunday mornings, when he helped me by running the vacuum cleaner in Stebbins's living room, Mrs. Cochran watched him and said, "He will be so good to you." Afternoons we walked in the hills.

My work was physically strenuous. Sheets were heavy when carried up- and downstairs. Kleenex and bobby pins were a chambermaid's nightmare because the vacuum cleaner inhaled them, clogging the works. Once, when there were few occupants, I ripped up the stair carpet and retacked it so the worn part was no longer on the edge of the steps but at the back, thereby keeping one of Stebbins's assets from depreciating for another year.

Teachers were pleasant occupants, most of

them tidy in their habits, except for a few bobby pins on the floor. Some of them took an interest in me, and when I said I was going to the University of Washington for graduate work but didn't know where I would live, one teacher said she had been a student there and had taken a room in the home of Miss Ruth Entz, a kindergarten teacher. She gave me the address. I wrote to Miss Entz, who replied that they had not rented the room for some time but would rent it to me for eight dollars a month.

My future was taking shape as I grew thinner and thinner from hard physical work. Jane invited me to come to Mill Valley for a couple of days when summer session ended. I accepted, which inspired Mother to write: "It is plain to see you are not anxious to see your parents." This made me angry. I had worked hard, and I was tired. I stood up to Mother and went to Mill Valley for two blissful days of good company and delicious food, including jam *and* butter on toast. Those two days gave me strength to return to Berkeley and board the train for Portland.

The train was unusually late, Sherwin-Williams covered the earth many times before we crossed the river, and when my parents met me, I remarked that the trip had been tiring. Mother said kindly, "You'll never have to go back again."

I was speechless. Did Mother think I was going to forget Clarence? Obviously, that was what she was counting on.

Mercifully, I had less than a month before school started at the University of Washington, where I was determined to live on the thirty-five dollars a month Mother said she and my father could spare, adding, "That little bit of money you earned isn't much help," a remark that cut deep when I thought of how hard the work had been.

Mother, a firm believer in my wearing red to attract men, had bought some bright red woolen fabric for a dress that I suspected she hoped would attract so many men I would forget Clarence. The way red flannel is used for frog bait, I thought with amusement.

I made the red dress before I took the train to Seattle. In a taxi on the way to the address on Miss Entz's letter, I saw that Seattle was a beautiful city of autumn leaves, lakes, and, in the distance, snowcapped Mount Baker. Elderly Mrs. Entz met me at the door and showed me to my room, which was small, with lavender walls and green woodwork. There were no windows but instead a glass door onto a balcony that looked into a cherry tree with yellowing leaves. The room was furnished with a narrow iron bedstead and, for a dresser, a piece of furniture so old-fashioned it had a cupboard for a chamber pot. My desk was a card table. The room seemed bleak, but it was also only eight dollars a month. It would do.

Miss Entz, I soon learned, was one of the kindest, most generous women I have ever known. The larger front bedroom was rented to a very old couple, the Coffins, who eked out a living on the husband's tiny pension from a Canadian university where he had taught history. He spent his days at the public library, where he was writing a history of the world. Mrs. Coffin cooked on a hot plate in a closet, but more often Miss Entz carried upstairs casseroles of stew or other hot dishes. If she hadn't, I doubt they would have had enough to eat. Whenever Miss Entz and her mother listened to classical music on the radio, I would find Mrs. Coffin, huddled on the stairs in the dark, listening. As I picked up my mail, an almost daily airmail letter from Clarence, from the newel post, she would say, "That young man had better save his money and buy an annuity." I didn't tell her that he was so extravagant he enclosed airmail stamps for my letters to him.

The School of Librarianship was in Suzzallo Library, a cathedral-like building that seemed elaborate after Cal's neoclassical Doe Library. In the main room of the library school we were assigned desks in predictably alphabetical order with our names neatly typed on white paper and pasted to green desk blotters.

There were forty-eight women and two men in the class, fewer than half direct from undergraduate work. Most had worked in libraries, saved money, and aimed for professional credentials and higher pay. The women referred to the school as the Cloister, and "the Missionary Spirit" was a phrase we often heard from instructors. I soon discovered to my chagrin that I had suffered needlessly through Advanced French Grammar. This university counted quarter, not semester, units.

The first quarter we all took the same classes. Fortunately, memories of the Ontario Public Library reassured me that being a librarian was more interesting than learning to be one. Cataloging exasperated me because I do not have an orderly, logical mind and could not see why it was important to snoop behind pseudonyms to find an author's true name. Why should Mark Twain always be cataloged under Samuel Langhorne Clemens with a cross-reference card from Mark Twain? Reference work was enjoyable. Each week we were given ten questions and the resources of the university library to find the answers in a sort of intellectual treasure hunt. Once, when I was wearing the red dress, a man who worked at the reference desk actually whispered, "You look like bait in that dress." He did not, however, turn into a prince.

Children's Work, the reason I was there, was under the guidance of a nationally known faculty member, Miss Siri Andrews, who had a round face and round glasses and wore a round silver medallion on a chain around her neck. Her courses took me back to my childhood. The slogan of children's librarians was "The right book for the right child." Adult Book Selection was taught by Miss Ruth Worden, a gray-haired woman who always wore navy blue suits and white blouses with touches of handwork on the collars, like baby dresses. She frequently used the expression "A rattling good tale" when referring to popular fiction. I looked forward to both Book Selection courses, but it was Miss Worden who gave me a feeling of inspiration for librarianship.

My days fell into a pattern as fallen leaves grew soggy, the weather damp and cold, and the morning air smelled of coal smoke as furnaces were fired up. After a breakfast of tomato juice, a sweet roll, and a carton of milk in my room, I walked a mile to Suzzallo Library. At noon I went with other students to the Commons, an inexpensive cafeteria run by the Domestic Science Department, where I drank another carton of milk and ate a sandwich cut into three parts, each with a different filling. I came to like the peanut butter and banana on raisin bread section and saved it for dessert. As we ate our meager lunches and watched drama students, scripts in hand, emote over cups of coffee with soggy napkins folded in their saucers sopping up spills, we discussed the finer points of cataloging and invented an imaginary series of books for our instructor to catalog: six volumes, each with a different editor or sometimes two, one of whom wrote under a pseudonym and the other under her maiden name, some volumes translated from foreign languages and requiring translator cards, each volume with a preface by a different author, etc., etc. This sent us into gales of laughter as each of us thought of an addition to make the assignment more difficult. Such is the sense of humor of librarians. We also had earnest discussions on the finer points of grammar.

Afternoons most of us studied at our desks until three o'clock, when we were granted the privileges of the faculty room, where we could have tea and two Ritz crackers for two cents. I looked forward to that tea and those crackers. About five I left school. Because other students lived in boardinghouses or at home, I sometimes ate dinner alone in the Commons, but more often

I chose a coffee shop or cheap restaurant on University Way, where I was fueled by creamed chicken on toast or hamburger steak. Then I returned to my lavender and green room to study and to write letters.

The high point of my day was picking up my mail from the newel post. Mother's letters were no longer amusing, but Jane, working for her teaching credential at Cal and reading blue books for an education professor, wrote long, entertaining letters about life at Stebbins, which I read and reread. Miriam, now married to Wilfrid, wrote from London. She was disappointed that British universities would not accept her Cal credits. Connie had moved to Berkeley to be near Park and was working at a San Francisco advertising agency while he earned his master's degree. Norma upset her family by insisting on marrying as soon as she earned her teaching credential rather than working a year first. Virginia wrote that she and Bob were getting married in the spring and wanted me to be a bridesmaid. Claudine felt teaching in a Portland suburb was an improvement over a mill town. Letters prevented loneliness.

Miss Entz must have guessed that my budget was stretched to its limit, for she said her mother would be glad to prepare me a breakfast for twenty cents on school days. Dear Mrs. Entz. She served me juice, hot cereal with raisins, a coddled egg, buttered toast with jam, and milk. I ate at a card table by the living room window while Heidi, their dachshund, sat up on her hind legs and wavered around on her long spine until she fell over, only to rise and try again. Those breakfasts sustained me through the year.

My eyesight became an increasing problem. The print in Mudge's *Guide to Reference Books* was even finer than my Shakespeare text at Cal. I began to have headaches. Once more I wrote home, more forcefully this time, and said I *had* to have glasses. This time Mother gave in. Perhaps my father interceded. I received the money and went to an ophthalmologist recommended by Miss Worden. There I learned that not only was I nearsighted, I had an astigmatism in one eye. When I put on glasses and walked out onto the street, I walked into a new world. I could see individual bricks on buildings, street signs were suddenly legible, lines on the sidewalks were sharper. My headaches left me, and I no longer squinted to read Mudge.

Then, at the end of the quarter, Miss Worden called me into her office. "Miss Bunn, you have done excellent work in Book Selection," she said, "but I am giving you a C because you looked bored."

I was speechless. Graded on my facial expression—I couldn't believe it. I may have been tired or hungry, but I was *not* bored. If her course had been Cataloging, I might have understood, for teachers of Cataloging are probably used to students looking bored. I don't know what I said, not much, and left her office as quickly as possible.

In the 1930s students did not rebel, probably because we were afraid to. We had too much at stake and, in our eagerness to prepare for security and a better future, were much too humble. When in the 1950s students began to rebel at Cal, I recalled a number of injustices to students and wished my generation had had the same courage. I doubt if any student today is graded on a facial expression, has graduation depend on composing an original tap dance, or is required to write twenty-four pages on "Plato: Teacher and Theorist." Cal's dreaded English Comprehensive has been abolished.

Except for my grade-C face, which did not expel me from graduate school, my grades returned to my pre-Cal A's and B's. The second quarter, we chose our field of librarianship. Miss Siri Andrews, a precise and thorough teacher, limited her classes to six students, who met in her office.

She gave us a project we worked on the rest of the year, designing a children's room in an imaginary public library in a town of ten thousand and selecting the basic book collection. We began by searching for articles on the number of books desirable for the population, the average size of books, the length of shelves to hold them, the arrangement of furniture. Then we selected books by classification, reading all the reviews we could find, typing cards, with notes and sources for each book, working in a small room full of clattering typewriters and walls lined with donated books the university did not know what to do with. One title I recall was *Men, Marriage, and Me,* by Peggy Hopkins Joyce.

When Christmas vacation came, I went home to Portland. Clarence had worked overtime so he could come to see me for a few days. This meant his first meeting, or confrontation, with Mother, which I dreaded. Dad and I drove to the station to meet him, and when we walked through the front door, Mother, smiling, made an entrance from the kitchen. She was wearing the pink dress she had made for me and that I had mentioned I had worn the night I met Clarence. I had left it in my closet when I went to Seattle. I was shocked and then angry. When I was alone with

Mother, I demanded to know why she was wearing my dress.

"It's the only thing I have to wear," she said.

This made me even angrier because, even though her wardrobe was limited, it was not true. What was she trying to accomplish? I have often wondered.

It was an uncomfortable time. Clarence was courteous, and Mother made some awkward attempts at conversation but quickly saw she could not manipulate him as she had Gerhart.

Dad was generous about letting Clarence drive the car, so we went everyplace I could think of to go. New Year's Eve we went out to dinner with Virginia and Bob. This time it was Virginia's turn to be shocked. Her mother had reserved the table next to ours for herself and Virginia's father. I suspected she wanted to look over the man I had imported from California. After dinner, when we were alone, Clarence slipped a cigar band on my finger and told me that someday he would replace it with a real ring. I still have the cigar band.

Christmas vacation was not an enjoyable time for any of us, and I was glad to escape into cold, blustery Seattle, where a gale sweeping across the campus was sometimes so strong I could lean into it and its force would support me, an experience I found exhilarating. All Seattle weather, no

217

matter how raw, was exhilarating after four years of California's blander climate.

Snow fell. "Mother Hulda is shaking out her feather bed," I wrote to Jane. This was a reference to a German folktale from Miss Andrews's course in Storytelling, in which we had to stand in her small office and tell to the class different types of stories—myths, legends, folktales, and modern fairy tales. Facing the sardonic looks of our peers in a small room was disconcerting, but when we went off to a branch of the Seattle Public Library, we found telling stories to children much easier because we could see pleasure on young faces.

Winter calmed and faded, the sun shone, and walking to the campus under trees sending out leaves was vitalizing. When the cherry tree outside my glass door was in bud, it was time for the class to divide and go off for a month of practice work. Several of us went to Portland, where I lived at home and against my will was involved in being a bridesmaid, while the others lived in a small hotel near the library. I was eager to do well in practice work and pointed out to Mother that although Virginia and Bob were good friends, being a bridesmaid took time and was an avoidable expense. Mother dismissed my argument by saying that this was something she and

Dad wanted me to do. Mother loved weddings, and I disliked arguing with her, so I became a bridesmaid.

Virginia, a most considerate bride, chose shades of pink for our dresses because her matron of honor had been married in a pink dress that she could use again. Virginia chose a similar pattern, and her Depression bridesmaids set to work on yards of pink chiffon, which slipped and slithered as we sewed.

Practice work, I was sure, was going to be much more interesting than struggling with chiffon, and I approached with eager anticipation the library that had meant so much to me. Weather, however, presented a problem. After a gray and dismal winter, the sun melted the clouds, the sky was blue, trees and flowers bloomed, birds twittered, and children played outdoors. They did not come to the library.

Collectively, the librarians who supervised practice students were kind and even entertained us with a luncheon, but my first week in the children's room of the main library was uncomfortable because the children's librarian was hard put to keep me busy. I read shelves, which meant seeing that books were in correct order, the most boring of library tasks. I was handed stacks of catalog cards to alphabetize, work I tried to make last as long as possible. Whenever a child entered, I offered to help find a book that he or she might enjoy and sometimes succeeded, unlike another student, to whom a little girl said, "Excuse me, but I think I can find a book faster myself."

I spent my lunch hours finding sandals, having them dyed to match my dress, meeting other bridesmaids in a shop that made us hats, pancakes with roses made from material from all our dresses surrounded by ruffles that matched our own. Mother also gave me errands, "since you are overtown." All I really wanted to do was sit down during my lunch hour.

During my next two weeks, in the branch libraries, rhododendrons bloomed, and the weather was still glorious, beckoning children from houses and schools but not enticing them to the library. I enjoyed the children's librarian in the first branch. She picked me up at home and drove me to the library and took me out for hamburgers for lunch. But what was she to do with me? She handed me a stack of catalog cards and said, "Sit here with these in your hands so that old bag will think you're doing something. Just keep away from her." The "old bag" was the librarian in charge of the branch. The children's librarian took me off to visit schools to escape the librarian's watchful eye.

When I went to the next branch, the sky was still cloudless, and Mount Hood was a pristine white cone. The children's librarian was pleasant but downhearted. She told me that when she first started to work in Portland, an older librarian said to her, "My dear, you look so young and fresh, and before you know it you will be wearing bifocals and arch supports." This children's librarian was looking for another position.

My first day I was to work from one to nine. The branch librarian immediately accosted me with "Did you bring a lunch?" Well, no, I hadn't. I assumed that I could get something to eat in a neighborhood coffee shop. She sighed and said, "Well, I guess I can take you out someplace." I felt like a nuisance.

I was disappointed and disillusioned by my experiences in the Portland Library Association, as the library was called at that time, before it became the Multnomah County Library. There was, however, one glorious day at the end of my month that restored my faith, a day on a bookmobile on its trip up the Columbia River Highway with a brisk, friendly librarian. Farmers' wives who waited with armloads of books greeted us like old friends, and while I checked out the new supply of reading material for their families, the librarian recorded requests to be brought on the next trip. We stopped at a sawmill town near Bridal Veil Falls where workers, wives, and children, all friendly and eager, came aboard. On the way back to Portland we stopped at Governor Meier's summer mansion, overlooking the Columbia River. The smiling servants came out to exchange their books. It was a beautiful, encouraging day that restored my faith in librarianship and left me with a lasting interest in bookmobile service.

In the midst of all this were wedding preparations, the selection of a wedding gift, the rehearsal dinner, and finally the wedding. When the bride's mother appeared, she, too, was wearing a long pink dress, but hers was expensive, with a pleated skirt that gave Virginia's bridesmaids, by contrast, a loving-hands-at-home look. On the way home afterward Mother "talked over" the wedding the way she had once talked over my high school social life: who attended, what they wore, who said what to whom. The next morning I posed on the front lawn in my pink chiffon with my still-fresh bouquet. The neighbors came out to watch, and one told Mother, who told me, that "Beverly looks terrible, her health all gone."

Once more I was glad to escape to Seattle.

In a few days Miss Worden called me into her office. She had the report on my practice work on her desk. She took off her glasses, pinched the bridge of her nose, put them on again, and told me what had been written about me. The librarian in the central children's room recorded that I was slow in filing; the "old bag" said she did not believe I was interested in children's work; the librarian in the second branch thought I was in poor health because I leaned on things. Leaned on things? I did have a pair of new pumps that pinched and probably leaned on something while I wiggled my toes, although I could not recall having done so.

I was devastated. All my years of ambition and hard work seemed wasted. I thought of Dad borrowing on his life insurance, Mother's sacrifices while she cared for my grandmother, all the creamed chicken I had eaten in the last months, all the kind people who had helped me along the way. The Portland Library Association, which had meant so much to me for so many years, had rejected me. I was exhausted, a complete failure. Miss Worden was nice about it, though. She let me go into the faculty rest room to dry my tears in private.

Next Miss Andrews called me into her office. I

dreaded facing her and decided to speak first. "I didn't do very well in my practice work, did I?"

She smiled and said, "I would like to see you start in the Los Angeles Public Library system. They are looking for a children's librarian and are willing to waive the residence requirement for you, but you would have to go to Los Angeles to take a civil service examination. Could you do that?"

Well! Suddenly I felt much better. Miss Andrews had faith in me, and as far as I was concerned, her opinion was the most valuable. I said I would see what I could do. Since I was so close to my goal, I felt I could ask my parents for a loan because I could repay it as soon as I was working. I wrote home and received a reply from Mother by return mail. They could not afford to lend me the fare to Los Angeles. I did not believe her. My father had received several small pay raises from the bank, and Mother received a monthly amount from my grandfather's estate for my grandmother's care and almost nonexistent expenses. Mother's motive was to keep me as far as possible from Clarence.

As I look back on this episode, I feel I should have asked Clarence for the money, but at that time, in the world in which I had grown up, this would have been a shocking thing to do. It was proper to accept airmail stamps, but money—never. Sadly I told Miss Andrews a trip to Los Angeles was impossible.

The semester was ending. We wrote model letters of application in case we could find a position to apply for. Miss Worden corrected them. She then spoke to the class and asked us not to accept positions that paid less than one hundred dollars a month "because we don't want to lower the standards of the profession." She added that this did not apply to Canadian students, who could not expect to earn a hundred dollars a month.

Miss Andrews called me in again and asked if I had enough money to get home. I did, just barely, but as it happened, I had a narrow escape. Forgoing commencement exercises, I packed, secured my typewriter in its crate, I hoped for the last time, said good-bye to Miss Entz and her mother, and called a taxi. When it arrived the driver told me he was no longer allowed to carry trunks. I must have looked so dismayed that he said, "I'll take a chance." He carried my trunk, which had very little in it, and my typewriter downstairs and stowed them in his cab. When we reached the depot, I held aside enough money for my train ticket and gave him all the rest, which wasn't much. The tip for his kindness probably amounted to about thirty-seven cents. He was nice about it, and without a cent to my name, I boarded the train for Portland. A Bachelor of Arts in Librarianship diploma would soon arrive in the mail. I was free of school, ready to go on with my life. All I needed was a job.

A Job and a Wedding

"Not one more cent," said Mother, and I agreed. Accepting money meant she could control me. Then she showed me a record of the cost of my college education. That hurt. I don't think she meant to be unkind, but I felt she begrudged the money even though I had managed on very little and had earned what I could. I resolved, when I had children, I would give with a loving heart.

Clarence braved my family once more, and during his few days in Portland, Miss Worden wrote of two vacancies, one in Tacoma, Washington, and one in Klamath Falls, Oregon. When I tried to type letters of application, I was so tense my fingers refused to hit the right keys. Clarence typed them for me, we mailed them, and went off on a picnic. We picnicked every day he was in Portland. Mother tried to give the appearance of friendliness, but her planned subjects of conversation lacked both warmth and spontaneity.

When Clarence left, I found some comfort in the sweater I was knitting for him with yarn we had chosen and he had paid for. My applications were not answered. With no job and no money, summer and possibly my whole life loomed like an oppressive cloud. Friends were equally dejected. Jane wrote that she was discovering there were no openings for English teachers who had minored in history. Only Virginia, the bride, was happy in her new home.

Each day of that early summer of 1939 seemed longer than the day before. The care of my grandmother was growing more difficult and Mother more depressed. Then Mrs. Klum suggested that Claudine and I spend the rest of the summer at Puddin'. Perhaps she was tired of having an adult daughter living at home. Mother, who did not need the added stress of a discouraged daughter, was glad to have me go. Dad promised he would drive out to the cabin with any mail from a library or from the university. He gave me money for my share of the groceries, money I was sorry to have to accept.

Claudine and I reverted to our high school

summers, swimming, reading, knitting, carrying our water, cooking on the woodstove. During the week we waylaid the man who serviced the juke-box to make sure he left recordings of Artie Shaw, Benny Goodman, and Tommy Dorsey. Weekends we danced with farm boys or city boys who were camping and earning a few dollars picking beans. As I listened to the clang of horse-shoes, the shouts and splashes from the river, and smelled the wood smoke and coffee of camp-ers and picnickers, the stress of five Depression years of college drained away, and I began to feel like myself again.

Then early one evening early in August, our car came bumping down the road. Mother and Dad were smiling, and Grandma, who would not leave the house without her hat and gloves, sat in the backseat looking frightened as the car jounced over potholes. Mother waved a letter. "There's a vacancy in Yakima," Dad said as he climbed out of the car.

"Where's Yakima?" I asked, and learned that it was a town in central Washington, hot in sum-mer, freezing in winter. The chance of a job! Who cared about the weather?

Back in Portland, I sent off a letter of applica-tion, adding, at Mother's wise suggestion, that I could come to Yakima for an interview. An answer came by return mail, Dad took a day off, and we drove over two hundred miles up the Washington side of the Columbia River and through brown hills to a town of about ten thousand people with fruit orchards to the west, dry rolling country to the east, and dominated by a monument to the Depression, the rusting skeleton of an unfinished fourteen-story hotel. The thermometer in a filling station where I changed into a white suit in the rest room registered 110 degrees. Dad dropped me off at the Carnegie library, where I was interviewed in the children's room in the humid basement by Miss Helen Remsberg, the librarian, and by the entire library board. Feeling presumptuous, I inquired about living accommodations even though I did not have the job. Miss Remsberg told me that one staff member lived at the YWCA, where she shared a kitchen.

Two days later I received a letter saying I was hired to work six hours a day in the children's room and two hours in the adult department beginning September 1 at a salary of one hundred ten dollars a month "because living was higher east of the Cascades." I was rich! Or soon would be.

Dad arranged for me to take out a seventy-five-dollar bank loan to get me through the first month until payday. I packed the remains of my shabby college wardrobe and, leaving behind my cumbersome typewriter, boarded a bus bound for Yakima and independence. When I arrived, however, I was told there were no vacancies at the Y for more than a few days. What to do? I bought a newspaper, consulted advertisements, and saw that my soon-to-be riches would not stretch to cover apartment rent. I finally found a boarding-house run by Mrs. Johnson, a single woman, thin and intense, who showed me a large pleasant room with an outside entrance and an old-fashioned library table, just the place for writing children's books on the portable typewriter I planned to buy as soon as I paid off my bank loan. I would share a bath with Mrs. Johnson, who slept on a couch in the dining room. On the evenings I worked at the library she suggested I eat dinner at Wardell's Percolator, a restaurant close to the library and noted for pies. I rented the room, expecting to stay only until there was a vacancy at the Y.

My first dinner in the boardinghouse was a shock. All the boarders were men: two from the Washington State Employment and Security Office, two younger men who were clerks for the Cascade Gas and Light Company, a sturdy old man who dug graves, and one or two others. They were as surprised as I. Conversation was friendly but strained, and after a dessert of ice cream made with canned milk, I fled to my room to write letters. This went on for several evenings until Charlie Walker, an older man who worked at the employment office, knocked on my door and asked if I wouldn't please come out and share the living room. Then the gravedigger brought me a bouquet of dahlias, the colors of jewels, from his daughter's garden. After that I felt more at home. The men called me Bunzy, except when I made what I thought was a sophisticated black dress. Then they called me the Widow.

Perhaps because I thought my stay was temporary, my parents did not object to my living in a house full of men. Clarence, familiar with boardinghouses, now says he felt I would be protected. I was. Charlie referred to the two men from the gas company as the "young Upshots" because one of them confused "upstart" with "upshot," beginning sentences with, "The upstart of the matter was . . ." On hot September evenings after work, the Upshots invited me to swim in an irrigation ditch. The swift current gave me a delightful sensation of being an excellent swimmer as it carried me downstream. I walked back.

During the time I lived in what Charlie called "Mrs. Johnson's caravansary," some men moved out and others moved in. One man who rented the downstairs front bedroom was so disliked by the other men that whenever he started upstairs to the bathroom, one of them would pop out of his room and beat him to it. Amused, I asked Charlie why. He merely said, "He has a dirty mind." He did not stay long. Dinnertime, which Charlie referred to as the Take Your Hand Off My Knee Literary Club, was full of laughter, but no one put his hand on anyone's knee. Several of the boarders supplemented our diet with trout, venison, and pheasant. Times were hard, and Mrs. Johnson appreciated the contributions to her table but asked us not to mention them outside the house. As I ate the game, I felt like a Pilgrim.

The first morning, as I climbed the library steps to report for work, I need not have been so nervous. The staff was welcoming. Miss Remsberg, I soon learned, was firm, kindly, and fair. When she reprimanded me she always began with the word *fetish*. "I don't want to make a fetish of printing, but you must improve yours on registration cards." She once reprimanded me for referring to "my department" by saying, "Miss Bunn, no part of the library is any staff member's private property."

Miss James, the cataloger and reference librarian, had a look of antique elegance as she came to work with artificial violets pinned to her fur collar and wearing matching purple gloves. She had a serious, orderly mind, and I am sure she considered me frivolous. We three professional librarians and Mr. Royer, the janitor, were always called by our surnames, all others by their given names: such was the hierarchy of librarianship. Charlotte, in charge of circulation, grew beautiful flowers for the library and always included a bouquet for the children's room. She kept me alert, for it was she who caught any errors I made. There were others: Hazel, a widow who worked part-time, a WPA woman who mended our tattered books, NYA girls who shelved books.

And then there was Berneita, an assistant and the only staff member to call me by my first name. From practical experience she knew more about books and children than I, but she was always tactful, willing, and enthusiastic. Whenever I was swamped with children checking out books, I had only to push a button that set off a buzzer upstairs, and Berneita, smiling and eager, came flying down the steps.

The children of Yakima. I shall never forget them. In a one-library town, the children's librarian meets all sorts of children: bright, healthy children of doctors and lawyers, children of unemployed millworkers, sad waifs whose poverty-stricken parents were past caring, garden-variety middle-class children such as those I had grown up with. At first many children puzzled me by calling me what I understood as "Stir." Then Berneita explained that they came from Catholic schools and were in the habit of addressing their teachers as " 'Ster," short for "Sister." French Canadian children laughed at my pronunciation of their names. To them "Lemieux" was pronounced "Lamear."

Individuals stand out in memory. One was a junior high school girl with red-rimmed eyes who had read every book of fiction in the children's room. The labels "teenager" and "young adult" had not yet placed young people in a separate social class. I took her upstairs and introduced her to the staff members, who helped her find adult books. A shy, shabby little girl presented me with a bouquet of lilacs. "Did these grow in your yard?" I tactlessly asked. "No, I just picked them," she answered. Wilma, Hazel's daughter, always brought her little brother to story hour, where they sat in the front row, their bright, interested faces an inspiration to a storyteller. A desperate father, furious because his son owed four cents on an overdue library book, shouted at me that his son's teacher had brought the class to the library and encouraged the children to take out books, so she should be responsible for the fine. I could have argued the point but instead quietly told him to forget the whole thing. The look of shame on the boy's face was too much to bear. I never saw him again.

Most vividly of all I remember the group of grubby little boys, nonreaders, who came once a week during school hours, marching in a column of two from nearby St. Joseph's School. Their teacher, 'Ster Bernard Jean, said their textbooks did not interest them and perhaps library books would tempt them to read. I soon learned there was very little in the library the boys wanted to read. "Where are the books about kids like us?" they wanted to know.

Where indeed. There was only one book I could find about kids like them, kids who parked their earmuffs on the circulation desk in winter and their baseball mitts in summer. That book was *Honk, the Moose,* by Phil Stong, a story about some farm boys who found a moose in a livery stable. All the boys liked that book because it fulfilled another of their requirements. It was funny. As I listened to the boys talk about books, I recalled my own childhood reading, when I longed for funny stories about the sort of children who lived in my neighborhood. What was the matter with authors? I had often wondered and now wondered again.

Children applying for their first library cards gave original answers to the question "What does your father do?" One little girl answered promptly, "He mows the lawn." Another girl gave the question serious thought before she said in triumph, "He types." Her mother, who was waiting to see how her daughter answered, explained with amusement, "He's an attorney."

Then there was a six-year-old girl, who, when I asked her father's occupation, answered, "He's a cat skinner."

"Does he stuff them, too?" I asked.

"No," said the child, impatient with the stupid librarian. "He skins *cats!*" she insisted.

I gave up, wrote "Cat skinner" on her application, and handed her a library card.

An NYA girl who was shelving books approached me timidly and said, "Pardon me, Miss Bunn, if you don't mind my saying so, a cat skinner is a man who runs a Caterpillar tractor."

Payday! One hundred and ten whole dollars that I had earned myself. When I received my first paycheck, I went downtown on Saturday night, a busy, colorful time in Yakima when Indians, many of the women with papooses on their backs, came into town from the reservation. I window-shopped, thinking of all that I could buy but settling on underwear and pajamas, which I never had enough of because they didn't show. I had money left over to start a savings account. After a few more paydays I paid off my bank loan and bought, *finally,* a portable typewriter for writing children's books. The trouble was, I didn't have time to write them. I made one attempt at writing a chapter about Puddin', but soon found I had too many other things to think about—letters to Clarence, stories to learn for story hour, books and library periodicals to read. Most of my evenings I read, read, read. There was so much I needed to learn, so many books to become acquainted with.

I could not forget my desire to write. When a publisher's representative from Macmillan came to the children's room and told me I looked like someone who could write a book, and if I ever did, he would like to send it to Macmillan for me, I was so flattered I let him take me to lunch, an incident I did not mention to Miss Remsberg, who was cool toward book salesmen. "I am not going to let salesmen select books for the library," she often said.

Saturday story hours began the end of September. I was to tell stories for three weeks of a month, and Berneita would take over the fourth week. The first week I had an attack of stage fright even though I had rehearsed two stories at home and in the half hour granted me in the staff room just before story time. Unfortunately, Miss Andrews had trained us to rehearse in front of a mirror, which did not help. In the staff room mirror, my hair, my lipstick, my appearance suddenly seemed all wrong.

As I was about to face my audience, Charlie walked into the children's room and presented me with a gardenia to celebrate the event. That gardenia gave me courage, and the story hour was a success in spite of the distractions of adults standing at the back of the room to listen, borrowers going in and out, fussy infants. I learned to concentrate on the faces of the children and to shut out everything that was going on in the room.

With the help of one of the Upshots I began to learn stories quickly. He enjoyed reading aloud. After he read the story I had chosen, I told it back to him while he prompted me. Soon I no longer needed his help. Not only did I tell stories in the library; in summer I told them in parks, where I competed with shouts and splashes from swimming pools. *The Five Chinese Brothers,* by Claire Huchet Bishop, was the most popular of the sixty-two stories I learned while in Yakima, and I told it many times. In 1939 and 1940 the Dionne quintuplets were in the headlines, which may have been one of the reasons children so often asked for the story about "the five Chinese twins."

Not all my storytelling was successful. I still cringe at the memory of my first visit to a small school outside Yakima's city limits. Using bus fare from the library's petty cash, I rode with my armload of books to the end of the line and enjoyed a pleasant walk the rest of the way on a road lined with sumac turning red in the autumn sun. My repertoire was limited, but I felt secure in my preparation of a story for the first graders, *The Wedding Procession of the Rag Doll and the Broom Handle and Who Was in It,* by Carl Sandburg. In the classroom I introduced myself and began the story, which contained such lines as "They chubbed their chubbs and looked around and chubbed their chubbs again." The words nearly froze in my throat. The class, children of migratory workers, all looking blank, staring at me as if they thought I was speaking a strange language. The expression on the face of the teacher standing at the rear of the room was no help. Somehow I got through that story, but that visit taught me always to find out something about an audience before speaking.

Other visits, to six public schools and two Catholic schools, were more successful. Children always made me feel welcome, possibly because my visit freed them from arithmetic or spelling, and I enjoyed introducing children to books. One small boy laughed so hard at my rendition of *Horton Hatches the Egg* that he fell out of his seat. When I stopped at an interesting point in a book talk, someone always asked, "What happened next?" and the rest of the class wanted to know, too.

There were other library activities that required preparation at home and prevented me from writing. Once a month I took over the library's weekly radio broadcast; classes walked to the library for instruction in the use of the card catalog; during Book Week I spoke to assemblies at the two junior high schools; and before school was out, I visited the elementary schools once more to talk about the summer reading club, an event probably more educational for a new librarian than for the children.

To earn a certificate, each child had to read eight books of suitable reading level and tell me about them. No taking the easy way out with picture books allowed. Everyone who joined was given a card with a picture of a clown holding eight balloons. After telling me about a book, the reader was given a colored sticker to cover a balloon. When school started in September I visited schools once more to hand out certificates to proud readers of eight books. Listening to Yakima's children tell me about the books they had read gave me valuable insights into the children and their reading.

While the atmosphere of the children's room was always lively, the two hours a day I spent in the adult department were quite different. The Depression was even more in evidence. The reference room was a haven for old men who came to read the newspapers we hung on wooden sticks. On rainy days one man dried his socks on the radiator. Housewives came for escape reading, a struggling writer for advice; so many people sought answers for a puzzle contest that they hoped would win them fortunes that we finally had to refuse to answer contest questions. Some people could not afford to pay two cents a day on overdue books and left empty-handed while we recorded their fines on tiny slips of paper pasted to their registration cards. They could not renew library cards until all fines were paid, a system that worried the whole staff, for it denied books to people who needed them most. When I left Yakima, Miss Remsberg was conferring with the city attorney to see if the system could be changed.

My tasks in the adult department were varied: registering new borrowers, finding books for readers, telling people they could not bring their dogs into the library, answering reference questions. Berneita explained that if a question asked over the telephone had an embarrassing answer, I could go into Miss Remsberg's office to say, for example, that "whales suckle their young." I soon learned to respect the Department of Agriculture bulletins, which were easy to use and invaluable in locating the period of gestation in goats or the cure for cabbage blight.

One seeker after knowledge asked me if there wasn't an older librarian who could find the answer to her question. I called Miss Remsberg, who explained with amusement that I was a library school graduate and well informed on the latest in reference work. Another time, when I found an answer, the borrower looked at me with skepticism and took the same question to Miss James, who looked up the answer, the same answer I had found. Even though my youth did not inspire confidence in everyone, I once wrote gloomily to Jane that in another year I would be a quarter of a century old.

There was another aspect of library service, not

taught in library school. This I thought of as Fear of Taxpayer. When reading book reviews, or especially books, during lulls, the staff always kept a pencil and a pad of paper slips at hand. Otherwise a sharp-eyed taxpayer might think we were enjoying ourselves. Discarding battered books also brought on Fear of Taxpayer attacks. In those Depression days a WPA worker mended torn pages with rice paper, replaced ragged spines with buckram, on which she lettered author and title with white ink, and protected them with shellac, and did what she could to hold books together. Libraries at that time did not have plastic to protect books' original jackets. Children's books too far gone for library shelves but still hanging together, more or less, were given to teachers from rural schools too poor to buy books. What to do with the rest? If they were sent to the town dump, they were sure to be seen by a taxpayer, who would complain that the library was throwing away books. If Mr. Royer tried to burn them, the glue in the bindings gummed up the furnace. Once Miss Remsberg solved the problem by asking me to make the smelliest, most tattered books worse. I ripped bindings and poured ink on pages. She then presented the books to the library board, and with official approval to back us up, we sent the books to the dump.

Because Yakima was so isolated, small events took on excitement out of proportion to their importance. When Sally Rand brought her feather fans to Yakima, the elderly gravedigger horrified Mrs. Johnson by inviting her to go with him to see her dance. Mrs. Johnson went, but not with him. I did not go, but I heard earnest discussions about whether or not Sally Rand was really naked behind her fans. Miss Remsberg's comment was "Well, I suppose she's part of the American scene."

The day nylons appeared on the market, the library staff went out in their lunch hours to buy the miracle stockings—reputed to dry in twenty minutes if rolled in a towel. The wonder of it all! When *Gone With the Wind,* originally a long movie with an intermission, came to Yakima, the whole town turned out. In the library the stack of reserve cards for the book was several inches thick.

One morning I received a telephone call at the library. It was Bob telling me that Virginia had died of a ruptured appendix. I was stunned. They seemed to have so much, to be so happy, and now Virginia was to be buried in her wedding dress.

Fall turned to winter. On rainy nights when I

worked until nine, a car parked in front of the library often blinked its lights, a signal that one of the men from the boardinghouse had come for me so I wouldn't have to walk home in the rain.

As the weather grew colder, an open-air ice rink opened a few blocks from the boardinghouse. On my Friday afternoon off, I rented a pair of skates and took a lesson, wobbling around the rink on the arm of an instructor. When I told this at dinner, the Upshots laughed. Who needed lessons to skate? Determined to learn, I bought a pair of figure skates and a season ticket to the rink, an act that gave me an attack of Depression guilt because these were for fun, not survival. To my surprise, in my new skates, whose leather was not softened by wear, I skated off without a wobble. I then made myself, on Mrs. Johnson's sewing machine, a red skating skirt with red bloomers. "It's Miss Bunn!" children shouted, surprised at seeing a librarian in a short red skirt. I skated alone on Friday afternoons, and evenings I sometimes skated with the Upshots. When I worked until nine o'clock, we often skated until midnight. A timid skater who could not risk breaking bones in those days before medical insurance, I found exercise both soothing and stimulating as I went round and round to *The*

Skater's Waltz or Bonnie Baker singing "Oh Johnny, Oh!"

The temperature dropped even lower. As I walked to work, the heavy fog that settled over Yakima froze and fell like dainty snow. Then real snow began to fall, and the ice rink had to be swept frequently. Skating in falling snow is exhilarating, but I soon changed from my short skirt to ski pants. Ski pants! I actually had money for ski pants, but of course I bought them on sale.

At Christmastime, Clarence traveled by train and bus to Yakima. In my eagerness to see him I went to the station much too early, fidgeted until the bus pulled in, and there was Clarence, in person, right there in Yakima. I took him to the boardinghouse, where one of the men who had gone home for Christmas had offered him his room. We sat on the living room couch, and as the radio played, Clarence produced a small velvet box, opened it, and slipped a diamond engagement ring on my finger. We kissed and without speaking rose and began to dance to the music of the radio. Before he returned to California we decided to marry the next December in San Francisco.

I let several months go by before mentioning my ring to my parents. As I expected, when Mother received the news, she wrote in anger, which left me depressed. I worked out my feelings on the ice rink.

The next June, Miss Remsberg and I planned to attend a library conference at Timberline Lodge at Mount Hood. Urged on by the Upshots, I decided to be brave and fly to Portland, and one of them drove me to the airport so he could actually see the inside of an airplane. The plane took off, bumping down air currents down the windy Columbia River Gorge to Portland, where Mother and Dad were excited to meet someone getting off an airplane at the Swan Island airport.

When I told them that Clarence and I planned to marry in December, Mother looked sad, but I was shocked by Dad's anger. Although I knew he was not enthusiastic, he usually could see my side and be understanding and supportive. Now I realized that because Mother wrote all the letters, I had not known the depth of his feelings. They refused to announce our engagement, and the next day I was glad to escape by bus to the conference at Mount Hood.

To me the highlight of the conference was seeing Dell McCormick accept the Young Readers' Choice Award for his book *Tall Timber Tales,* which I had used with success with my little troop of nonreaders. I was awed to hear a real author speak and would have been even more awed if I had known that someday I would win the same award and win it more than once.

After the cool mountain air in Oregon, the summer heat of Yakima was dehydrating. Life was speeding up. I told Miss Remsberg that I was leaving in December, so she wrote to Miss Worden at the university about a replacement. Miss Worden wrote back, "I can guess what Miss Bunn's next move will be."

Talk of war was increasingly serious. World War II had begun in Europe. Charlie was haunted by his memories of the First World War, when he had left his premed course at the university to volunteer with his fraternity brothers. He had been assigned to caring for the dead on the battlefields of France, an experience so devastating he was unable to continue his medical studies when the war ended. That summer of 1940 he suffered so badly with allergies he finally had to go to the Veterans Hospital in Walla Walla to recover.

In September I was given a two-week vacation (with pay!). After a few days in Portland, where Mother and Dad were cool toward me, I fled by train to Sacramento, where Clarence had managed to take his vacation at the same time. We spent a few days with his mother, who had retired and lived in a cabin in the foothills of the

Sierra. With her car we drove to the Bay Area, where I was greedy for the sight of the Campanile against brown hills and the silhouette of San Francisco across the bay. Clarence stayed with his sister in Oakland or his brother in San Francisco, and I slept on a too-short couch of Connie and Park's, who were now married. I was sad to miss Jane, who had found a job, not as a teacher, but as a secretary to a high school in Southern California. Clarence and I attended the Exposition on Treasure Island, danced at the Mark Hopkins, and much too soon it was time to return to Yakima and the library.

One day a couple of weeks later I received a telegram at work. Expecting news of someone's death, I opened it with shaking hands and read, COME BY AIRLINER STOP WILL WIRE AIRFARE STOP CLARENCE. I had worked my year, and Clarence had been reluctant to see me leave after my vacation. I knew Mother and Dad would never give me a wedding. Suddenly I was angry and weary of trying to appease them. Why not get married now? Life was fragile; Virginia, the happy bride, had died so suddenly. Why should Clarence and I wait any longer?

I consulted Miss Remsberg, who advised me to go ahead because my parents would not change their feelings until after we were married. She gave me an extra day off, but cautioned me that our marriage must be kept secret in Yakima because Berneita was getting married the same week and "Yakima will not stand for two married women on the staff."

Miss Remsberg also said that she did not understand why the children had liked me so much; I treated them the same way I treated adults. Of course. That was the way I had wanted to be treated as a child.

I pulled myself together and flew to Sacramento, where Clarence met me. We drove in his mother's car to Reno, where, with his younger brother and sister-in-law as witnesses, we were married at the Church of Our Lady of the Snows. The next day I flew back to Yakima wondering how I was going to break the news to my family.

As it turned out, I didn't have to break the news. A couple of evenings later, when I was alone in the house, the telephone rang so persistently that I answered, although I did not usually do so. It was Mother. "We see you and Clarence are married," she said.

How on earth . . . ? "Yes," I answered. "How did you know?"

"We read it in the *Journal,*" she said. "And now people will think the worst."

I recall very little of the conversation except

that I said, "How did you expect us to get married? You wouldn't give us a wedding."

Mother answered, "A priest wouldn't come to our house, and we could never go to a Catholic church. I dread what people will say." Mother never forgot the neighbors. If neighbors counted months on their fingers, they were mistaken. It was fifteen years before we had children, twins to make up for lost time.

But how did news of our marriage get into Portland's *Journal?* We had both given fictitious residences. Soon two letters arrived. Mother wrote scathingly of two people trying to hide in a town "the whole world has its eyes on." She also enclosed a three-line newspaper clipping date-lined Reno announcing the divorce of someone from Portland and our marriage with my last name given as Dunn. Mother said I had killed her. As it turned out, no one in Portland recognized our names in the paper. Dad wrote that I need not stop in Portland when I moved to Sacramento.

Worn-out with years of controversy, I responded with a brief note agreeing it was best I not stop in Portland. Mother, in need of saving face, then wrote that I should stop in Portland for an announcement party. This was the last thing I wanted, but I reluctantly agreed to help save my parents embarrassment. I then got on with my work at the library and having neglected dental work done so that I would not burden my new husband with the expense.

Why hadn't I rebelled sooner? Because I felt sorry for my parents, trapped as they were by the Depression, struggling to give me an education. I appreciated all they had done for me and felt indebted to them, but now, at the age of twenty-four, I felt I had a right to make my own decisions.

When Mother was in her eighties, she told one of my cousins, "I wanted Beverly, and Clarence wanted her, and I finally had to let her go." She never did let me go, not really.

In those last months in Yakima, war was on everyone's mind. The young men at the boarding-house registered for the draft, an event I recall by the seats of their pants as they leaned over the dining room table searching for their draft numbers in the newspaper. Clarence wrote that he had drawn a high number—what a relief! At least we would have some time together before he had to go off to war—if the United States became involved in war. Somehow, it seemed hard to believe.

My last weeks as Yakima's children's librarian went quickly. Berneita and I constructed a gingerbread house for the children's room, and I told Christmas stories. I was sad about leaving the staff and the work I enjoyed. As the day of my departure grew closer, the men in the boarding-house surprised me one evening at dinner by giving me a set of linen dish towels and several pieces of silver in the pattern I had chosen.

Berneita felt I should have some sort of celebration, so she gave me an announcement party in the new home her husband had provided. She was proud of showing off her silver and Spode, and when dessert, wedding bells of ice cream, was served, each supported a catalog card announcing our marriage. The heading, in proper library form, read:

Cleary, Beverly Atlee (Bunn), 1916—

I don't recall the title we gave the book, but I do recall hoping that someday there would be author cards with the same heading in the catalogs of schools and libraries.

My second announcement party, in Portland, was a sad little affair held on a wild, stormy night. Not all the guests could come in such weather. Clarence sent Mother and me corsages, but Mother resisted wearing hers because "it wouldn't do for me to be too dressed up in my own home." Dad and I were tense, but nervous, exhausted Mother managed to smile and tell everyone what a fine young man Clarence was and how pleased she and Dad were over our marriage. It was a difficult evening, but Mother had saved face with the neighbors.

Le déjeuner sur l'herbe, *library-school style*

A tired bridesmaid, "health all gone"

An application picture taken the week we were married

Story hour in the park, temperature about 110°

One of the Upshots cooling off in a puddle on the lawn of our boardinghouse

Charlie Walker, a dear and lasting friend from the Yakima boardinghouse

Claudine at the beach the weekend she met her future husband

The Sather Gate Book Shop

We started life together, Clarence and I, in his bachelor apartment on the ground floor of a Victorian house near California's state capitol, where he now worked in the state controller's office. After Clarence carried me across the threshold in proper bridegroom fashion, I saw hanging above the bed a picture of a weary Indian drooping on horseback. The title was *The End of the Trail.* I took the picture down and hid it under the bed, which annoyed the landlady.

I continued to write to Mother and Dad once a week as if nothing had changed. Mother laboriously answered, hunting and pecking on my old typewriter letters that she tried to make cheerful but that made me sad. She could not hide her depression.

Clarence said he wanted me to choose a place to live, and after looking at Sacramento apartments, we finally moved into another apartment in the same building, which I liked to think of as picturesque. It, too, was on the ground floor but was light, airy, and looked out on the backyard and a gardenia tree. I had not known that corsages grew on trees.

One morning, as I struggled to learn to cook on another three-burner-over-an-oven stove, I found a suspicious-looking insect in a cupboard. I captured it and presented it to the landlady, saying, "Is this what I think it is?"

"Oh, my dear, it's a *cockroach,*" she said as if I were fortunate to be able to present her with such a gift. "They are *so* easy to get rid of." She gave me a saucer of borax and told me to put it on top of a cupboard. I did, and never saw another cockroach.

Early in 1941 the Bureau of Internal Revenue notified us that we owed twenty-five dollars in income tax. If we didn't pay, our property would be attached. Twenty-five whole dollars? Why? Clarence, calmer than I, explained that because we had both worked the year before, our combined salaries made us eligible to pay income tax. Since our property consisted of an armchair we had bought for five dollars and had reupholstered, a card table, and a floor lamp bought with S&H green stamps, we joked about what the government would do with our property, and paid up.

Then Clarence received an offer of a better position, with the U.S. Navy Cost Inspection office in San Francisco.

"It's a plot!" cried our eccentric landlady. "Working in the state capitol is an honor, and someone is plotting to get his job. Don't go!" We went.

In San Francisco we found a two-room apartment that, in our innocence, we did not realize was on the edge of the Tenderloin. Whenever I stepped out on the street alone, men cruising in cars tried to pick me up. This did not stop me from walking downtown to have lunch with Connie or other friends or climbing over Nob Hill to take a WPA course in block printing. On Polk Street, old men with red noses and red hands shucked oysters. Fruits and vegetables strange to me were displayed along the sidewalks. I compared prices and splurged on a papaya, the first we had ever eaten. My experiment with fava beans was a failure, but I was more successful with salsify. For the first time in my life I took an interest in food and cooking. Saturday evenings we went to small French or Italian restaurants for dinner. Afterward we went to a theater on Powell Street that showed double features for twenty-five cents.

We enjoyed San Francisco, but when Clarence was assigned to work in the navy office at a shipyard in Alameda, we decided to move closer to his work. Knowing little about Oakland, we took a train to the Fruitvale district, which was joined to Alameda by a bridge across the estuary. We found an attractive, unfurnished three-room apartment on the top floor of a Victorian house. The landlady lent us a bed, and we moved in. The large kitchen window looked out on eucalyptus trees at the end of the dead-end street, or cul-de-sac, as real estate advertisements call such a street. A hill rising behind the trees was crowned with a spooky-looking house that could have come from a Charles Addams cartoon.

Neighbors, except for one quiet Japanese family, were mostly Italian and Portuguese. The first question women asked me was "Did you go to college?" When I admitted I had, an invisible curtain dropped between us. When I walked to the branch library and returned with an armload of books, I felt as if the neighbors were eyeing me with disapproval. Didn't this woman have anything better to do than read?

There was no time for loneliness. I shopped for

a few pieces of furniture, and we traveled by public transportation to visit friends in Berkeley. Then one Saturday night, as we waited for a bus, we were struck by a thought: *We could buy a car.* We were so used to the Depression and traveling by public transportation that such an extravagant thought had never before entered our minds. After searching want ads we found a secondhand Chevrolet coupe for sale just half a block away. We bought it, and Clarence started to teach me to drive.

Because we needed furniture and because I felt I should keep up with children's books, I went to the Sather Gate Book Shop in Berkeley, where Quail Hawkins was a well-known seller of children's books. I introduced myself and found her instantly enthusiastic about hiring a children's librarian to help during the Christmas rush. She took me upstairs to meet Mrs. Herbert, the store manager, an elderly woman with glasses so thick she made me feel like a mouse caught in the gaze of an owl. This formidable woman was inclined to dismiss me because I had no selling experience. "But she knows *books!*" cried Quail, her cheeks beginning to flush.

"But we don't know if she can sell," insisted Mrs. Herbert.

"If she knows books, she can sell them," countered Quail, her cheeks now flaming with emotion.

Quail won out. Commuting by two buses and a streetcar, I went to work for eighteen dollars for a six-day week in the store that had the largest collection of children's books west of Chicago. Quail, I soon learned, was a rapid, omnivorous reader with a retentive memory, a love of books, and a passion for persuading others to read them.

Bookselling was full of surprises. First of all I learned, but had trouble remembering, to stand back when punching the cash register so the drawer of that hostile machine would not hit me in the stomach. I learned that information could be located without the use of the card catalog. I learned that it was easier to persuade a customer to buy a book than it had been to persuade a library patron that a book was worth borrowing. When a grandmother asked for a book for a twelve-year-old, I soon caught on that the child was usually only ten but was "as smart as a twelve-year-old," at least in Berkeley.

From Quail I learned to disarm disgruntled local authors who felt the store was neglecting them because their books were not displayed in the front window or who had counted their books on the shelves the previous week and returned

269

to count again and complain that we had not sold a single copy in the entire week. We smiled and said, "We were hoping you would come in. Would you mind signing some of your books?" Authors never minded. Someday, when I found time to write, I promised myself, I would never behave in bookstores like Berkeley's local authors.

The pace was fast. "Count the little brown things," cried Quail my first morning at work. Baffled, I asked what she meant. The Little, Brown publisher's representative was coming, so the number of copies of each Little, Brown title in stock must be counted and marked in a catalog so there would be no delays when Quail gave her order. The time of publishers' reps was precious, she explained. To count, we climbed the ladder in the stockroom and crawled on our hands and knees to reach books behind books on lower shelves. In between, we waited on customers, replenished stock, and wrapped books for gifts. Little Golden Books, which sold for twenty-five cents, were a popular item. We wrapped endless copies of *The Poky Little Puppy* and *Saggy Baggy Elephant,* but no matter how busy we were, somehow the catalog was counted by the time the publisher's rep arrived.

The work was exhilarating, and the customers in the university town were pleasant—except one. That customer was a world-famous scientist who shall remain nameless. He strode through the store and demanded my name. When he got it, he roared in a voice that must have reached Telegraph Avenue, "Mrs. Cleary, show me the most beautiful book published this year."

"How old is the child?" I asked, trying to find a starting place.

"Mrs. Cleary," he boomed, "I want the most beautiful book of all."

I do not recall the book that satisfied him, but I do recall the difficult forty-five minutes I spent trying to produce it while other customers fumed. When I checked the charge account of the world-famous scientist, I had the embarrassment of asking him to please step up to the office—there was a problem with his credit.

I was to work as Christmas help four different years, which, except for the first year, have mostly blurred into one. Business expanded and so did my pay—ultimately, to twenty-five dollars a week when four of us manned the children's department, and there was no room to stand back when we punched the cash register. Two episodes stand out in memory, besides hiding in the stockroom when the world-famous scientist entered.

When a customer telephoned and asked us to hold a book, the last in stock, until she could come in, we wrote her name on a slip of paper and set the book by the cash register. Sara, one of the saleswomen, noticed that invariably other customers wanted that book. She began to choose slow-moving books and insert slips of paper on which she wrote, "Mrs. Wogus will call." The book always sold even though Mrs. Wogus was a cow in Walter R. Brooks's "Freddy" books.

Then there was the year Quail was offered a large discount on five hundred copies of Margaret Wise Brown's *Little Fur Family,* a tiny book with a jacket made of fur packaged in a box with a hole in the center that gave the Fur Child pictured on the lid a real fur stomach. Mr. Kahn, the owner of the store, bet us a box of candy that we could not sell five hundred copies by Christmas. We sold all five hundred, explaining five hundred times that the fur jacket was made from the pelts of kangaroos, varmints in Australia, and that no good American rabbits had been sacrificed. Mr. Kahn paid up.

Of my four years as Christmas help, that first year, when Quail and I were the only employees in the children's department, remains most vivid of all. One Sunday afternoon, Clarence and I were listening to *The Mikado* on the radio when the broadcast was interrupted by a bulletin:

Pearl Harbor had been bombed by the Japanese. "I'll be damned!" said Clarence.

"Where's Pearl Harbor?" I asked.

We stayed by the radio the rest of the day, and the next morning went to work as usual. That week the store, with almost no customers, was in a state of nervous confusion. Quail, who had a brother who was a naval officer stationed at Pearl Harbor, was on the verge of tears, hoping for a telephone call with news from him. As we all waited with her, we passed the time catching up on stock work and counting catalogs in what seemed like slow motion while we talked of black-out curtains and bombings. Then Mrs. Herbert paid us a visit to keep us on our toes. "Girls," she said, "we must sell even though we are at war." As we were wondering to whom, she turned to Quail and said, "Darlin', we do not accept personal calls at work." When Quail finally heard over the store telephone that her brother was safe, the sales staff rejoiced for her.

After work, Clarence and I nailed layers of newspapers over our kitchen windows in place of blackout curtains, listened to President Roosevelt's "date which will live in infamy" speech, and prepared hasty dinners. At night, when air raid sirens sounded, we leaned on the bedroom windowsill, looked out into the black night, and listened to the drone of circling planes. Dogs, upset by sirens, airplanes, and darkness, barked until the all clear was sounded and lights came on again.

Gradually customers trickled back to the bookstore. Children should not be disappointed, they said, and one indignantly added, "I do think the Japanese might have waited until after Christmas."

Quail came down with flu, and I was left to face the department alone. When she returned, Mrs. Herbert, a kind woman in her own way, took me aside and whispered, "Darlin', we don't discuss our salaries, but I am so pleased with your work I am raising your pay from eighteen to nineteen dollars a week." This was the same woman who wrote the date on every light bulb installed so the store could be reimbursed if bulbs did not live up to their guarantees. She also required us to show her a very short pencil stub before she would issue us a new pencil. Money was still tight in 1941.

After Christmas, still unscathed by bombs, I returned to being a full-time housewife. I stood in line at the meat market, but when my turn came, all the butcher had left to sell was pig tails.

Gas rationing ended my driving lessons. From our kitchen window I watched the Japanese family, laden with bundles and suitcases, quietly leave their home and climb into a taxi on their way to the Relocation Center. It was a sad scene; they were such gentle, courteous people. Our landlady gave us a plot in the backyard for a Victory garden, which I enjoyed, remembering, as I had been taught in grammar school in Portland, to rotate our crops and to plant legumes to replenish nitrogen in the soil.

College friends married, had babies, were called into service, returned to their homes, or disappeared, leaving us to wonder where they had gone. Someone sent a newspaper picture of the Upshot who had been eager to see the inside of an airplane. He was sitting in a BT-14 training plane at Randolph Field. In spite of his high draft number, we were not sure how long Clarence would remain a civilian, and we did not feel it was time to start a family. I had no intention of going back to Portland to live with my parents. We finally decided it would be best if I were settled in a job. Now all I had to do was find one.

I Meet the Army

Like the younger sons in folktales I had told in Yakima, I set forth to seek my fortune, beginning with the Oakland Public Library. I flunked the physical examination because the doctor said I was too nervous to meet the public. I did not let him discourage me.

My next stop was the Department of Employment, where I half expected to be sent to a shipyard to become another Rosie the Riveter. Instead I was sent to apply for a library opening at Camp John T. Knight, which turned out to be a compound of barracks, a chapel, and one-story white shoebox buildings in the Oakland Army Base on the edge of San Francisco Bay. There I learned that another librarian, older than I, had been sent from the San Francisco Department of Employment. She was given the title of Post Librarian, but since librarians were in short supply, Xenophon P. Smith, Chief Librarian of the 9th Service Command, did not want to let one slip through his fingers. Would I consider sharing the position with the title of Junior Hostess? A Junior Hostess would normally work in a service club, but since there was none at Camp Knight, funds were available. Why not? I was amused by my title, which reminded me of the song "Ten Cents a Dance." This time I passed the physical examination with the army doctor's gentle comment "Why, you're frightened." I met the Special Service Officer, who was responsible for library and recreation services. He introduced me to Colonel Alfonte, an Old Army Commanding Officer, who told me that listening to the men talk was more important than library work, but I must never ask questions. I had a feeling that life in the Yakima boardinghouse full of men had been basic training for my new army life.

And so I went to work at raw, windy, bleak Camp Knight. Even sunny days began with cold fog pressing down on white buildings, gray sidewalks, and mud. When the sun did come out, the men whistled tunes from *Oklahoma!,* and the camp often had a sickly-sweet smell of coconut as copra from the South Pacific was unloaded on its way to becoming soap. At one end of the block-long street, ships loading explosives flew red flags. On one side of the library a railroad track of flatcars was loaded with tanks, guns, explosives, landing craft, Jeeps, the machines of war. In daylight the cars stood motionless, but during the night their loads disappeared, and by the time we came to work, another trainload awaited its voyage to the South Pacific. Camp Knight was not a place to lift the spirits.

The post librarian and I worked in a small room in a building designed to be a mess hall but temporarily used as a day room, the army term for recreation room. As I listened to the men, new words, which Clarence defined for me, were added to my vocabulary. I did not use them. Pool balls clicked, Ping-Pong balls, as James Thurber was to say, *gnip-gnopped,* and the jukebox played over and over the men's two favorite songs, something about "Why don't you do right and get me some money, too?" and a burlesque song that contained the line " 'Take it off, take it off,' cries a voice from the rear." The children's room of the Yakima Public Library seemed a long, long way away.

In a few weeks book-filled shelves lined the walls. The pool table, Ping-Pong table, and jukebox were moved out and replaced with long tables and pewlike benches. When we remarked to the colonel's wife that we thought a library needed some comfortable chairs, Mrs. Alfonte, loyal to the Old Army, said indignantly, "Some of the finest generals in the army have sat on those benches." Perhaps that explained why West Point officers were always so erect. Slumping was impossible on those straight-backed benches.

Then our Special Service uniforms arrived. They were blue gabardine suits with shoulder patches that looked like the end of an open book with pages of different colors representing branches of the service. "The Rainbow Division," the men called us. I was lucky enough to find a pair of British Walker shoes that buckled on the side and were appropriate with a uniform. The camp was so muddy that polishing them seemed a waste of time, but I did shine them once in a while. My shoes must have bothered the men, who were required to keep their shoes polished at all times. One of them presented me with a can of Kiwi polish. After that I treated myself to professional shines, and my shoes gleamed and passed the men's inspection, which my stockings did not.

My one remaining pair of nylons had to last the Duration. For work I found some handsome,

I thought, cotton mesh stockings imported from England, where they were probably worn for hiking on the moors but were suitable to wear with my British Walkers. I wore them until the men began to ask, "Do you have to wear those stockings?" I did not care to paint my legs as some women did, so my next choice was rayon stockings, presentable if worn wrong side out so they didn't shine, but with feet so badly shaped that pulling them on was like putting my feet into paper bags. They did not dry overnight, and all through the war our shower rod was draped with damp rayon stockings. The men said no more.

The white shirts we were required to wear with our uniforms were also a problem. They were difficult to find and were usually rayon, sure to disintegrate in a short time if sent to a commercial laundry, which in wartime could not promise when they would be returned. Even though housekeeping was simplified by a lack of furniture, I resented ironing shirts in my limited free time until I discovered I could cut the work in half by wearing shirts wrong side out on the second day and keeping my jacket buttoned. No one noticed. Then overcoats arrived. They were made of such coarse stiff woolen fabric ("shoddy," Mother would have called it) that when I sat down on the A train, the overcoat did not sit with me. The collar rose above my ears.

On the mornings when I opened the library, no matter how cold and blustery the weather, men, both black and white, were waiting to use the Coke machine. At that time the army was segregated, but our library was not. Rank and race made no difference to us.

The men of the United States, uprooted from their lives by lottery and thrust into the Quartermaster Corps or Military Police, were a revelation more enlightening than travel. I was astounded at the variety of men who found themselves at Camp Knight. A furrier from Marshall Fields in Chicago remarked, "Humph, split skins," when a corporal's wife walked in wearing a fur coat. A professional gambler from Georgia confided that payday gambling with young soldiers was "jest like rakin' in the leaves" and asked for our help in filling out applications for postal money orders so he could send his winnings home, where he was buying an apartment house. A bootlegger explained how to smuggle liquor into the dry state of Kansas. Several law school graduates from City University of New York hoped somehow to get onto the Judge Advocate General's staff. A man whose job in civilian life had been dyeing the marbleized edges of dictionaries explained how it was done. Another man had done a stretch for robbing a Chicago hotel. Men from crowded cities reminisced about their lives in the "C's," as they called the Civilian Conservation Corps.

The men seemed equally amazed by one another. I overheard a black man telephoning his wife on the library's pay telephone say, "They sez they's Creoles. What the hell is Creoles?" Men from big cities spoke contemptuously of "those farmers" and looked down on fresh-faced small-town boys from the Midwest who saw war as adventure. This did not sit well with me, once a farmer's daughter, and I finally snapped at one man, "You eat, don't you?" After a moment of startled silence, he said apologetically, "I never thought of it that way."

The language of the army fascinated me. Once when I was hurrying to the Post Exchange to buy a sandwich before the only sort left was potato salad on white bread, a private caught up with me and said, "Jeez, you shoulda been in the infantry, the way you pick 'em up and lay 'em down."

Our feet grew cold on the cement floor as men showed us pictures of their families and confided, in their various accents, plans for the days when the war, which had only begun, would end and they could return home. When one man who had been promoted from corporal to sergeant asked if I knew where he could get his new stripes sewn on his blouse, I volunteered to do it for him. After that I sewed on new stripes several times a week. Private First Class stripes were the most difficult because they tended to stretch or bend while I was sewing.

Companies were moved out of camp and replaced by others. Often men from the East came straight to the library to ask, "How far is it to Hollywood?" When told it was about four hundred miles to the south, they asked in disbelief, "In the same state?" When we said that California extended about the same distance to the north, they often said "Jeez" in disbelief.

Once the camp had for a brief time a detachment of men who censored mail for the Army Post Office. They were ordered to skim through letters going to men overseas but not really read them. "You can't help reading them," one man said. "You get so you watch for certain letters." Another said, "It seems like some women have no shame."

I felt sorry for the men, most of whom worked in shifts around the clock loading and guarding ships. Many men had no consideration for those who had to sleep in the daytime and did not lower their voices. Radios played night and day. One man told me he became so angry he picked up a radio, held it over his head, and dropped it on the floor. We did not disturb exhausted men who came to the library and fell asleep on the new couches. These couches had mysteriously arrived to replace the pewlike benches, leaving us to wonder what became of those benches. Were they shipped to the South Pacific so men would sit up straight in the jungle?

This seemed as reasonable as some of the army's orders. When an order came from Post Headquarters—"The men will attend the movie, and the men will enjoy themselves"—the men laughed about it. When a man imprisoned in the guard house, probably for the usual offense of swearing at an officer, requested a book on mathematics, we sent him one. A sergeant returned it. The Bible was the only reading material permitted in the guard house.

Then one day it was announced that the camp was to have a gas mask drill. Everyone would be issued a mask and be required to walk through a building filled with gas. The day came, but the library staff had not been given masks. "What about us?" we asked, only to be told we were not included in the drill because we were paid from different funds.

Life on the home front was difficult. When we worked a five-day week, I could sometimes go to Mill Valley to visit pregnant Jane, whose army officer husband was in Italy, but when the government decreed that we must work six days a week, I no longer had time for the trip or any other recreation. Going to work meant either waiting for an unreliable bus or walking thirteen blocks to an A train, where passengers were curious about my uniform with its jaunty hat, which also bore the rainbow insignia. "What kind of uniform is that?" I was often asked. One woman wanted to know, "Just who do you think you are in that getup?" Another asked what I was all togged out for. At the army base I had a choice of walking a cold, windy mile to the library or riding in a truck. Going home was easier. Clarence, concerned about my traveling through an unsafe West Oakland neighborhood on the nights I worked until nine o'clock, applied to the ration board for extra gasoline so he could pick me up after work. He was granted enough to come for me every day. We often stopped to eat at one of the several small restaurants on the way home.

When I worked nights I packed a spartan meal, usually a Spam sandwich and a piece of fruit. According to Army Regulation 210-70, librarians and hostesses were the equivalent of captains.

This should have entitled us to get meals in the officers' mess across the street, but we were denied this right, a decision apparently made by a Red Cross volunteer who impressed officers with her wealth. She always carried five hundred dollars in cash so she could lend money to any man in need. That we could have complained by way of our library officer to Colonel Alfonte did not occur to us, and today I wonder why a volunteer was allowed to assume so much power. It was she who insisted the men wear uniforms instead of fatigues to the library because being in uniform would make them "feel better." We felt men should be entitled to use the library no matter how they were dressed.

Although I enjoyed listening to the men, I did not find Camp Knight a pleasant place in which to work. Almost no one wanted to be there except a few officers who had never had it so good. Enlisted men resented their officers and disliked their work on the docks. As one man told me, "When you stand guard all night, it seems like you hate the whole world."

One event lifted spirits. Not long after the library opened and Colonel Alfonte was transferred or retired, one of his successors was court-martialed for "making improper advances to the wives of younger officers." This was a great morale booster for enlisted men because it showed them officers were not always given preferential treatment.

Still, the library was an uncomfortable place. The post librarian understandably resented having to share her position with a junior hostess. I was doubtful about her abilities as a librarian because she disliked selecting books and left their choice to me, work I enjoyed. She also refused to catalog books. I did not mind taking over because I used a simplified system and used the authors' names on title pages. Mark Twain was Mark Twain. She spoke of "her" library, which irritated me after Miss Remsberg's lecture on no part of a library belonging to any one staff member.

The assistants were usually engrossed in personal problems and did not stay long. I missed the calm kindness I was used to from Miss Remsberg in Yakima, the friendly cooperation of the Yakima staff, and the companionship of Sather Gate Book Shop. Poor food, erratic transportation, irregular hours were beginning to wear me down. I was well paid by the standards of the times, but I had little need for money. In wartime, stores spread their merchandise thin or left shelves bare, and wearing a uniform six days a week, I had no need for more clothes. We could have used more furniture, if we could find any, but I would only have to dust it, and a rug would lead to a vacuum cleaner that would have to be run. A dust mop was faster. I had nothing to do with my checks but deposit them in the bank. Did I really need this job?

Then, after a bad case of flu, when I was about to give up, I received a call from Xenophon P. Smith telling me the Hotel Oakland was being converted into an area station hospital. He suggested I look the place over, and if I wanted the position of post librarian, it was mine. A job only a twenty-minute streetcar ride from home with no transfers—of course I wanted it, but when I went to the hospital, I found myself involved in the strangest interview that any librarian I have ever known has had. I was shown into the office of the commanding officer, who was leaning back in his chair. He misunderstood the situation and thought he was interviewing me. A huge man, tall and heavyset, he sat up, reached out, pulled me toward him so I was standing between his knees, gave me two pats on my bottom, and said, "So you're a librarian. You can have the job anytime you want it."

I stepped back and stared at him. All the men I had met at Camp Knight had been friendly, courteous, and proper. No one had ever touched me. I thought fast. By this time I had seen enough of the army to know that officers did not stay long in one post. I would take a chance.

The C.O., assuming the matter was settled because he said so, released my hand, sprang to his feet, and said, "Follow me. I'll show you where the library is going to be," and left the room with long strides.

"Run!" cried the secretary in the outer office. "Run, or you'll lose him."

I ran. This giant of a man led me down the hall and into the ballroom where I had danced when I was a student at Cal. Thus began a relationship of post librarian vs. commanding officer. He waved his hands and explained how the ballroom was to be divided, with Red Cross recreation offices at one end, a stage in the center, and the library and Special Service office behind the stage. "And the Dutch door to the library will go here," he said, pointing.

A divided door in which the top and bottom halves opened separately? "Why a Dutch door?" I asked.

"So the men can come to the door and ask for their books," he said. "We can't have them going into the library and getting the books out of order."

I was speechless. Then I thought of the rallying cry of the Office of Librarianship of the 9th Service Command: "Make adversity work for you." A rich opportunity of adversity lay ahead, if I could make it work.

My War with the Army

Traveling to work at the Oakland Area Station Hospital was much easier and much more interesting than my journey to Camp Knight. I walked two blocks to the number 14 streetcar, run by a very old motorman named Willy, who had been called out of retirement to serve during the war. Willy, glad to be back at work, took wicked pleasure in speed, and piloted his car over the uneven roadbed as if he were in a race. We bucketed around Lake Merritt, past the Hanrahan, Wadsworth, Pine, and Borba Funeral Home and a place that manufactured "The Laminated Shim That Pe-e-els for Adjustment," whatever that was, to stop directly in front of the hospital.

I was given a desk in medical supply, down the

hall from the morgue, where I could make out book orders while the ballroom was being converted. The administration correctly assumed that a librarian was entitled to eat in the officers' mess, a real treat after so many Spam sandwiches. The food was good, and we were often served steak. In wartime! I savored every bite of those meals even though surgeons came into the mess in their blood-smeared "scrubs." Enlisted men, suspicious of officers, often asked what I had to eat "in there" and were reassured to learn that officers and enlisted men were served the same food with one exception. Officers had salad.

I quickly revived from life at Camp Knight. My first obstacle was the Red Cross, which objected to my starting a library when its workers already circulated books from a small collection of donations. When I pointed out that the army provided both librarians and ample funds for books, the woman in charge of recreation told me I could have the medical library, but the Red Cross would continue to supply reading material to patients. I quoted AR 210-70 to the library officer, who consulted the C.O., who pronounced, "There will be one library in this hospital, and Mrs. Cleary will run it."

When partitions were in place, I moved from medical supply to the most poorly designed library I have ever seen. It was T-shaped, with the stage in the recreation room in one angle, the medical library locked in one arm of the T, and the circulation desk and the Dutch door in the other arm. Over the partition, in the long part of the T, was the Special Service office. The main part of the library made a detour around a thick pillar. Light came from two windows and a crystal chandelier suspended from a very high ceiling.

With the help of a sergeant who had been wounded on Attu and was on limited service, we opened the library with books piled on the floor. We solved the Dutch door problem by leaving both halves open, an act of disobedience the C.O. apparently never noticed, probably because he was so busy changing specifications for library shelves, which I had sent him and which he said would waste lumber in wartime. When his six-foot-long shelves arrived, they sagged under the weight of books. The C.O. humphed and snorted and ordered them rebuilt. But did he follow specifications? Of course not. He was the C.O., wasn't he? This time he had the shelves made the right length but so high we could not reach the top shelves. Most of them remained empty, wasting lumber all through the war.

Once the books were shelved, the sergeant was

assigned to other duties, and a civilian assistant was hired, a pretty girl named Judy with curly red hair who often said, "This is the best job I have ever had. I just *love* working in the library." Even though she was worried about a brother serving in the navy in the Pacific, she was always willing and cheerful. The Red Cross, now friendly and cooperative, gave its book carts to the library and assigned Gray Ladies to help in the wards. Most of these volunteers had sons or husbands in the service and were enthusiastic workers. Without their loyal help, the library could not have efficiently covered the wards in a six-story building designed to be a hotel.

The library was not the only part of the recreational facility badly designed. The stage had only one dressing room, the size of a closet, which was inadequate for USO shows. Since the library was closed evenings because ambulatory patients had little to do during the daytime but select books, we allowed the library to be used as a dressing room. I did not mind picking up bits of hula skirt when I came to work, but I did mind an unanticipated problem with the Dutch door. The lock was in the top half, and the Red Cross worker in charge of the evening's entertainment invariably went home with the key instead of leaving it with the sergeant at the entrance to the hospital. The bottom half could be opened without a key, and so, until the Red Cross worker with the key could be located, everyone had to bend low to enter the library. When the entire door was open, the library was so noisy that at night I went to bed with the click of billiard balls, the *gnip-gnop* of Ping-Pong balls, and "Cow-cow Boogie" pounded out on the piano still running through my head.

As the days grew shorter, the library grew darker. One high chandelier designed to flatter ballroom dancers was inadequate. I brought my college desk lamp from home for use on the circulation desk, but the patients could barely see the shelves. I complained to the library officer, who passed my complaint on to the C.O., who came to see for himself, humphed, and left. Before long, fluorescent lights, twice as many as needed, were installed and produced light so bright one man said, "When I come in here I feel like I am about to be beaten with a rubber hose."

Then one day inspectors from the Fire Department arrived. Ignoring me, they stood in the narrow space in front of the circulation desk, where one man pointed to the shelves opposite and said with authority, "A door can be cut through these shelves *here,* and steps built down *here.*"

Steps in front of the circulation desk for patients to trip over? And what about book carts and men on crutches? They couldn't get past steps. I interrupted. "Why is the door needed?" I asked.

"Fire Department regulations require two exits from a stage," the inspector said. "There is none on this side."

This suddenly struck me as funny. "But doesn't the front of the stage count as an exit?" I asked. "In case of fire, couldn't performers simply jump off the stage?" The men looked thoughtful, departed, and that was the end of that project.

One day an enlisted man came in and picked up the ancient Woodstock typewriter, which probably had been mothballed since World War I, and started out the door with it. When I protested, he said, "Sorry. There aren't enough typewriters to go around. I have orders to take this one."

Finally there came a time when I had to start a letter through channels to the commanding officer of the 9th Service Command on some minor matter. Because librarians were not allowed to write official letters in their own names, letters always began, "On behalf of the Commanding Officer . . ." and were signed by the post librarian and the library officer before being passed on to the C.O. Here was my chance. I wrote the letter in my neatest longhand, signed it, and turned it over to the library officer. "Why isn't this typed?" he demanded.

"Because the army took away my typewriter," I said.

He signed the letter and, with a hint of a smile, sent it off to the C.O. Before long I was called into the adjutant's office. "What is the meaning of this?" the major demanded, holding up the letter. "You can't send a handwritten letter through channels."

"They took away the library's typewriter, sir," I answered.

He handed the letter back to me. The typewriter was returned.

Next we faced the problem of dust in the army. The post library at Camp Knight had been "cleaned" by sullen prisoners from the guard house while an armed M.P. stood over them. With wide brooms the prisoners pushed the dust and grit from one end of the library to the other and then pushed it back again. We dusted the tables ourselves with dustcloths brought from home. No one worried about dust on books. The whole camp was dusty, and nobody cared.

Dust in a hospital was different. During weekly inspections the officer in charge looked for dust and found it. When I explained that dust on library books was inevitable, the officer went peacefully on his way until the day the C.O. conducted the inspection himself. Ah-ha! Dust on library books! The accompanying officer recorded our dust on his clipboard. The next day half a dozen cleaning women arrived to remove the books, dust them, and return them to clean shelves. The library was busy and the women were almost finished before I noticed they were shelving the books at random. When I pointed out that books should be shelved in order, they seemed bewildered. Then I understood—they could not read. Reshelving several thousand books was a daunting task, but fortunately sympathetic patients offered to help.

The C.O. not only wanted a dust-free station hospital, but wanted to command a dust-free regional hospital. "Keep the bed census up" was a remark often heard. On the C.O.'s orders, the bed census was kept up, and eventually he won out and became the commander of the Oakland Regional Hospital.

Before long, as I had anticipated, the C.O. was transferred. His last order to me was "Buy me a couple of Thorne Smith books out of library funds." I didn't do it.

The next C.O. was Colonel Harry Dale, a tall, thin, bald officer whose erect bearing indicated a

West Point background. The first time he entered the library, the men sat as if frozen. Colonel Dale looked around and said we should have a proper circulation desk instead of the beat-up old office desk we were using. "Go ahead and order one," he told me and added, "Is there anything else you would like to have?" I could scarcely believe what I was hearing.

There certainly was something I would like to have: a door that was not a Dutch door. The next day, carpenters arrived, measurements were taken, and a new door was installed, a perfect door that did not divide in the middle, a door divided into glass panes that diminished the noise from the recreation room and at the same time allowed men to see that the library was open. I thought loving thoughts about Colonel Dale every time I opened that door.

Another kindness of Colonel Dale that I particularly appreciated was his asking me, when the Special Service officer who was also library officer was about to be transferred, "What do you think is the chief duty of a library officer?"

After a moment's thought, I answered, "To say yes to whatever the librarian asks."

Colonel Dale laughed and asked me to choose any officer I would like to have. I selected a mild-mannered lieutenant who worked in the mess office. The moment a new library officer realized with horror that he had to sign for the entire library and was held responsible for all the books was always an interesting moment until I quoted AR 210-70 and assured him that all he had to do was sign papers. I took care of everything else.

Working on what the chaplain's assistant called the lunatic fringe of the army was fascinating, a view of the joys and tragedies of life. Babies were born, patients' bodies were mended, men died. One handsome young man requested a book on mathematics, and when I took it to him, we talked a few minutes. The next day I was shocked to learn he had died. When an army wife who had been hospitalized with high blood pressure gave birth to stillborn twins, her young husband sat in the library with his head in his hands for hours.

The case that caused the most excitement was an army wife who at dusk had backed into a spinning airplane propeller, which sliced off three pounds of her buttocks, shattered her elbows, and fractured her skull. Her husband, barely out of his teens, came every afternoon for weeks to read Western stories to her as she lay facedown. Everyone followed her progress with concern, and the staff was proud of its work when she was finally able to walk out of the hospital.

Italian cobelligerents, men who had been taken prisoner but were unsympathetic to Italy's part in the war and had volunteered to work for the United States, sometimes became patients. This irritated the men who fought in the Italian campaign. "We fought those guys," they said. The Italians were very much aware of their unpopularity. I went to a North Beach bookshop in San Francisco and persuaded the owner to sell the army about fifty paperback books in Italian, which the men were happy to find on the book cart. One homesick Italian admitted for an ordinary appendectomy looked so sad that the chaplain felt sorry for him and called on an Italian priest to come and visit with the man in his own language. Instead of being cheered, the poor patient went into shock. In his town in Italy a visit to a sickbed by a priest meant the patient was going to die.

A young gunner with the British Merchant Marine turned up at the hospital for several weeks. He was a handsome young man who admired the quality of American uniforms compared to his own. He was popular with girls, including Judy, but he soon married another American girl. He then learned, when his orders arrived, that he was being sent to Australia by sailing vessel. "Eyety dyes to Austrylia," he moaned. Almost as soon as he left, his American bride sought a divorce, which upset his family in England, who did not take divorce lightly and who somehow wrote to Judy about it. She was saddened by the letter and wasn't sure how she should answer. I suspected she was in love with him herself.

Almost every day enlisted men asked for the key to the medical library, and when we explained that it was for the use of medical officers only, the men usually grumbled, "What's the matter? Are they afraid we'll know more than they do?" I tried several times to persuade Colonel Dale to move the medical library, pointing out that according to AR 210-70, using my time to take care of it was a misappropriation of funds. Adversity did not work this time.

An army chaplain requested a book on flower arranging, a subject I had not expected to interest the army. I bought the most beautiful book I could find, and when I handed it to him, he remarked, "We teach little children to worship in beauty and then send them to Sunday school in church basements." How well I remembered. To my surprise, a number of men borrowed that book.

Men sometimes asked what prices were like "on the outside," as if the army were a prison. I telephoned Montgomery Ward and asked for a catalog, which we kept in the library. Someone was always studying it, and some men compiled lists from it as they dreamed of the future when they could return home.

And then there was the first lieutenant in the Engineering Corps. I shall call him Jimmy. Once Jimmy asked if we could think of a holiday that he could use as an excuse for sending his wife a gift. We consulted reference books and found that grouse-shooting season was about to open in Scotland. "Great," Jimmy said with a grin, and left, presumably to send his wife a gift appropriate for grouse shooting. Jimmy was full of fun. We made a game of quoting poetry to see if the other could identify it. I wondered if he had been required to memorize as much poetry in high school as I had. One day Jimmy said he was bored. Wasn't there some work he could do in the library? There was. To our surprise Jimmy shelved books, not only that day, but every day.

Several enlisted men said, when Jimmy was not around, "I don't get it. A first lieutenant shelving books." We didn't get it either; we were just thankful. We wondered what he was being treated for, but of course we could not ask. Then one day Jimmy did not appear. As we shelved books ourselves, we missed his help and his good humor. When Colonel Dale came in, I remarked that we missed Jimmy. The colonel said the entire hospital staff had been amused because the librarians were the only people in the hospital who could do anything with Jimmy. I was astonished, unaware we had been doing anything with him. The colonel explained that Jimmy had been held prisoner in the hospital because there wasn't much he hadn't done, from attempted rape to cashing bad checks. His wife had not heard from him for months. He had been given a dishonorable discharge and sent on his way. The next day he telephoned Colonel Dale to say he was broke and had no way of getting home to the East Coast. The colonel told him to start walking.

Most doctors, I soon learned, read history, biography, and mysteries. Men who broke their legs riding motorcycles always wanted Western stories. The psychiatrist requested books by Arthur Koestler. A man who said in civilian life he "sold jewels to rich old women" shared my pleasure in James Thurber. After the war I saw him doing just that, selling jewels to rich old women in I. Magnin. Enlisted men often asked for books by Donald Henderson Clark, an author I had never heard of. The 9th Service Command's library philosophy was "Give the men what they want." I ordered *The Impatient Virgin, Tawny,* and other

Clark titles, which the men pounced on, usually saying, "I didn't think you would have *these*."

Best-sellers were in demand, most of all *Forever Amber,* by Kathleen Winsor. When I saw the author's picture on the book jacket, I recognized a Cal student with whom I had shared Professor Lehman's course in The Novel and who had surprised the student body by marrying the captain of the football team. That book, written by a classmate, was a nagging reminder every time it crossed our new circulation desk that I, too, wanted to write—if the war would ever end, and I could find time.

That was one question I did ask Colonel Dale: "When is this war going to end?"

He answered, "The same time all wars end. When people get tired." It seemed to me everyone was tired. Men asked for the prophecies of Nostradamus to search for clues to the end of the war. There was no longer any need to look at pins on the maps posted in the hospital lobby. I could tell how the war was going by the faces of the men. Clarence's draft number was coming closer. He was called to the Berkeley High School gym for what enlisted men called "short-arm inspection." The navy had him deferred, and I dreaded long franked envelopes in the mailbox. Would they contain a draft notice or another deferment? Mother, whose letters grew more depressed, wrote asking if it wasn't time for Clarence to go. Judy's brother was killed in a naval battle. His C.O. wrote the family, "Nathan was a fine boy." His name was Aaron.

If Colonel Dale's prediction was correct, the war could not go on much longer. Although Clarence and I had no time for recreation, we were glad to turn our living room couch into a bed for transient relatives. Atlee, now a trim and handsome navy flier too tall for our couch, slept on it anyway. He could not tell us at the time, but we learned years later that his aircraft carrier had been kamikaze'd and was being repaired. His sister, Virginia, also turned up to sleep on our couch. She was married to a young man in the navy who was stationed on Treasure Island.

Then my grandmother died, my dear, gentle grandmother, who taught me to sew when I was five years old. Mother stopped to spend a night or two on our couch on her way to visit Verna, as well as her own oldest brother, who lived in Arizona. Seven years of caring for her mother had aged her. Her spunk was gone. I felt sad for Mother, who, although she had always been strict with me, had also been fun-loving until the circumstances of her life had eroded her sense of fun. The visit was peaceful, but I was careful to watch every word I said. Mother did not ask how much longer Clarence's civilian status would last.

Then, in 1945, on April 12, which happened to be my birthday, a patient came into the library and said softly, "Excuse me, Mrs. Cleary, but did you know President Roosevelt died?" I didn't. A terrible gloom settled over the hospital. "Now we'll never get out," the men said. Radios broadcast only classical music. No one played "Cowcow Boogie." Ping-Pong balls did not *gnip-gnop*.

Late in the afternoon of that terrible day, a big fat sergeant carrying a bouquet of red roses walked into the library. "Are *you* Beverly Cleary?" he angrily demanded. I confessed. "Jee-zus Christ," he snarled, and thrust the roses at me. "We thought these were for a patient and just about tore the hospital apart trying to find her." Clarence had remembered my birthday.

On May 7, Germany surrendered to the Allies, a morale-lifting day in the hospital. The men felt they were closer to going home—unless they were sent to the Pacific. Patients were discharged more quickly than usual, and their places filled with men with eerie greenish skins, the result of taking Atabrine in the tropics to prevent malaria. Others, who had picked up skin fungus in the jungles, looked like mummies. One man described to me his problems soaking his socks off his feet, infected with jungle rot. Another, a civilian whose eyesight was failing from starvation on the Bataan death march, told me of the death of his wife and child from dysentery. All this could mean only one thing: Hospitals in the South Pacific were preparing for a major battle.

Then the atomic bomb was dropped on Hiroshima. Stunned silence fell over the hospital. Colonel Dale came into the library as if nothing unusual had happened and returned his books.

"A whole city wiped out with one bomb," I said. "I think that is horrifying."

"No," answered the colonel calmly. "It will bring about the end of the war and save the lives of thousands of our men." It still seemed a terrible thing and a long way from the small atom-smashing cyclotron in the shack on the Cal campus that the Commonwealth Fellows had shown with such pride one evening only eight years before.

Japan surrendered. Sirens sounded, whistles blew. Patients whooped, hollered, and threw their toilet paper out the windows. Everyone left the library except the Chief of Medical Services, who calmly selected books as if nothing unusual were going on. When he finally left, I locked the door, went home, and fell into bed as exhausted as if I had been in a battle myself.

Men were quickly discharged except for a few very young newly enlisted men who wanted to read dog stories. Then they, too, disappeared, and the hospital was turned over to the Veterans Administration. I was asked to stay on, but when I went for a tour with the new C.O., watched him scrape the floor with a fifty-cent piece to show how slovenly the army had been in waxing over dirt, and saw him wave his arm around the library I had worked so hard on and say, "We'll get rid of most of this junk," I felt as if I were back with my original hospital C.O. I also knew that I was through with government library service. Later, when I met the librarian who took over for the Veterans Administration, she told me what a pleasure it was to inherit a professionally selected library. Junk, indeed!

The Post Library at Camp Knight in the hectic days when I didn't have time to get my hair done

Colonel Harry L. Dale, a kind, just, and humorous C.O.

The Oakland Regional Hospital, where I enjoyed supplying patients with books and where, when it was Hotel Oakland, I had danced when I was in college

Laughter in the Post Library of the Oakland Regional Hospital. Johnny, the British gunner, and Judy on the far left

Clarence amuses Kitty in front of our first house in the Berkeley Hills. Hannah said he was "debasing the cat with cheap tricks."

I was not strangling the cat.
He always tried to avoid
cameras, and I was restraining him.

I have no idea why I looked so roguish at a neighbor's house.

Clarence after he gained weight on my cooking and before he gave up smoking

Hannah looks on as I sign books at the Sather Gate Book Shop.

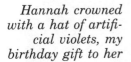

Hannah crowned with a hat of artificial violets, my birthday gift to her

Mother and Dad in 1949

Taken about the time I sent off my first manuscript

A House, a Cat, a Letter

Life as a housewife in a three-room apartment was a letdown after the stimulating work in the hospital. War had scattered friends, most of them now married and parents of infants, with little time for writing letters. Librarians I had met as a member of the Special Libraries Association asked if I would be interested in their libraries, but when I learned the work would consist of research handled by mail, I felt it would be too much like writing college papers. The postwar cost of construction prevented us from building a house on a lot we had bought during the war. Clarence was transferred to the university, where he was in charge of government research and development contracts. His travel time made our days longer.

For the first time since the war began, I went to Portland to see Mother and Dad and to admire Claudine's beautiful baby boy. Dad, who had aged, said little but was obviously more than happy to see me after such a long time, and Mother enjoyed serving ice cream and cake to my friends when they came to call. Then one evening when Mother and I were doing dishes, I remarked that now that the war was over, Clarence and I were thinking of starting a family.

Mother said, "Oh, this having babies is just a fad."

I managed not to laugh but pointed out that if people didn't have babies, the race would die out. But I wondered. Why had Mother made such a remark? Later, I asked her. Her tart answer— "Well, I said it, didn't I?"—left me wondering if she did not want me to have children.

When I returned from Portland, I told myself that if I was ever going to write a children's book, now was the time to do it. But when I sat down at my typewriter and stared at the paper I had rolled into it, the typewriter seemed hostile, and the paper remained blank. The longer I stared, the blanker it seemed. After years of aspiring, I found I had nothing to say. Maybe it had all been a foolish dream.

I kept busy making a braided rug to go in front

of our living room couch and, inspired by work I had seen in the Red Cross craft shop at the hospital, traveled to San Francisco to study wood carving with a retired puppeteer who lived in his studio over a former Chinese laundry. "That's nice," said one of the neighbors. "Gives you something to do." I carved trays, a sewing box, panels for a chest, and a mask intended to be a Greek god that turned out to look like Clarence with horns and a beard.

Then a brief pregnancy ended disastrously, leaving me pale, depressed, and lonely for the child we did not have. I had to pull myself together. To stop moping around feeling sorry for myself, I once more became Christmas help at the Sather Gate Book Shop. By then wholesale business had increased, and four of us, reaching over and around one another, manned the crowded department, serving customers and pulling library orders. There was no room to stand back from the punch of the cash register drawer. Credit cards were new, but machines for stamping names and addresses had not come into use.

I felt better being with people, and gregarious Quail, who collected people, invited Clarence and me to a party. I was fascinated by her rustic house furnished with antiques of no particular period. The living room windows were eighteen feet high and looked across a deck to a view of one end of the bay and to the bottom of a cliff, an abandoned quarry that Hannah, Quail's mother, had turned into a rock garden. I was even more fascinated by the mixture of guests of all ages: architects, writers, artists, publishers' reps, and bookstore customers whom Quail found interesting. That evening revived my spirits.

When we returned to our apartment, I told Clarence I wanted to move to Berkeley. *Now*. He agreed. The next weekend we drove aimlessly around the Berkeley Hills on streets where we had walked when we were students. Three blocks up a steep winding road from Quail's house, we came upon a FOR SALE sign in front of a privet hedge that hid a brown redwood house shaded by eucalyptus trees growing in vacant lots on either side.

We stopped, walked down the brick steps through a terraced garden, and knocked on the door. Within a couple of hours we had bought a five-room house clinging to the side of the hill and only ten minutes from Clarence's work. As it turned out, we had bought a house and a cat.

The naval officer who owned the house was being transferred, and the cat, a large, sleek tabby with a white vest, was destined for the Humane Society. Didn't we want a cat? No, we did not want a cat. Parting with their cat was so painful to its owners that we agreed to feed it for the ten days they would be staying with relatives. They agreed to let us paint the laundry while the house was in escrow, which horrified the real estate woman handling the sale.

We left a bedroom window open so the cat, who had simply been called Kitty, could go in and out. When we arrived with paint and brushes, Kitty ran to meet us with the saddest miaows I had ever heard, and when he followed us into the house, his desolate cries seemed to echo through the empty rooms.

"We're going to keep that cat," said Clarence, beating me to it. We did our best to console Kitty, who endured a lonely escrow, felt reassured when furniture arrived, and was quite at home when we moved in. Because he felt the house was his, he ruled us with a fur-covered paw of iron and proved to be a remarkably intelligent animal with a large vocabulary of expressive miaows, demanding praise when he presented us with a gopher, coaxing a young cat who was badly treated into the house to share his food. He recognized the sound of our car when it was two blocks away, and ran to the door to meet Clarence. He did not care to sleep in the laundry on cold nights, so he figured out how to open the door so he could make himself comfortable, after a thorough bed-jiggling wash, in the middle of our bed. We loved the neighborhood, we loved the house, we loved the cat.

We had discovered in the linen closet a ream of typing paper left by the former owner. I remarked to Clarence, "I guess I'll have to write a book." My ambition, refusing to die, was beginning to bloom again.

"Why don't you?" asked Clarence.

"We never have any sharp pencils" was my flippant answer.

The next day he brought home a pencil sharpener.

The trouble was, I couldn't think of anything to write about. Besides, I was busy turning our house into a home. We bought dining room furniture to go over the braided rug. I braided another for the living room from my army uniforms, Clarence's wedding suit, and other memories. Quail, always generous with hospitality, helped us make friends with neighbors whose houses were scattered among the eucalyptus trees.

But it was Quail's mother, Hannah, who became my special friend. She had been a newspaperwoman for the *Spokesman Review* in Spokane, Washington, as well as the mother of Quail and six sons. She was the first liberated woman I had

ever known, although I sometimes felt her libera-
tion had come at the expense of others. When
Clarence and I walked down the hill to Quail's
house for dinner, we often heard mother-daugh-
ter shrieks floating up the canyon, but by the
time we reached their doorstep, they were laughing at how ridiculous their argument had been.
Their relationship, although not an easy one,
seemed much healthier than my relationship
with my mother.

Afternoons I often walked down the hill to see
Hannah. Sometimes she invited me for lunch to
eat "dead party," her term for leftovers from entertaining. Hannah loved parties and, when telling about one, often said, "Life is a soap opera."
She liked young people, particularly if they were
creative, and often said, "Deliver me from my
contemporaries." I once found her in the garage
running sheets through the mangle and singing
at the top of her voice, "Seated one day at the
organ, I was weary and ill at ease." Hannah insisted on gracious living, and that included
ironed sheets even if she had to iron them herself. We drank instant coffee out of thin china
cups that rarely matched because Hannah, who
had an eye for antiques, felt that matching dishes
were uninteresting and middle-class. What mat-
tered was the quality of the china.

As we drank the dreadful coffee out of elegant cups, we engaged in what Hannah called "airy persiflage," but sometimes we were serious. Hannah once said, "You know, Beverly, you are afraid of your mother." I was startled, but I knew she was right. I sat, silent and thoughtful, looking out at her beautiful garden spilling down the cliff, and wished Mother had such a creative interest in her life. Hannah treasured every plant and even managed to persuade lilies of the valley to bloom in California by putting ice cubes on the plants in hot weather. For work on the steep slope she wore a big hat trimmed with corsage ribbons and pumps with three-inch heels, which she speared into the ground to keep from falling. "I dread the day when someone calls me spry," she said.

Mother and Dad drove down from Oregon to see our new house. "Why, this is luxury!" cried Mother as she walked down the brick steps. "We worked all our lives for a house like this"—an exaggeration because the Portland house was larger, with an attic and basement, was more solidly constructed than our little house, and they hadn't worked all their lives for it. They bought it when Dad sold the farm.

Dad's attitude was different. He took an interest in cineraria and other unfamiliar plants in our garden. He laughed heartily when we told how Clarence had spent half a day digging a huge thistle away from the corner of the garage, only to have a puzzled neighbor inquire, "Don't you *like* artichokes?"

I had asked my parents to bring us an old pair of andirons stored in the basement. Instead Dad insisted on taking me to Breuner's to choose andirons, fireplace tools, and a screen. "We had to work so long for ours," he said, and Mother agreed. My relationship with Mother was improving, but even so, the visit had its tense moments, and I was glad to return to furnishing the house.

To help pay for some of our new furniture I became Christmas help in the bookstore once more. One morning, during a lull, I picked up an easy-reading book and read, " 'Bow-wow. I like the green grass,' said the puppy." How ridiculous, I thought. No puppy I had known talked like that. Suddenly I knew I could write a better book, and what was more, I intended to do it as soon as the Christmas rush was over.

During that Christmas season, Quail was excited because Elisabeth Hamilton, children's editor of Morrow Junior Books and, according to Quail, the smartest editor in the business, was coming to speak at a library meeting in San Francisco. Quail, who had published a couple of easy-reading books and collaborated on two books for older readers, was eager to hear Mrs. Hamilton and asked her salespeople to go along if they were interested. Of course I went.

Elisabeth Hamilton was a tall, handsome woman who wore a white hat and told amusing anecdotes about her authors, which I found a bit disappointing when I had expected her to hand down Wisdom, but she had a presence that was impressive. After her talk, on our way out, I asked if she wrote a letter when she rejected a manuscript. She courteously replied to a question she must have heard too many times, "Only if the author shows talent but the book is a near miss."

On January 2, 1949, I gathered up my typewriter, freshly sharpened pencils, and the pile of paper and sat down at the kitchen table we had stored in the back bedroom. *Write* and no backing out, I told myself. In all my years of dreaming about writing, I had never thought about what it was I wanted to say. I stared out the window at the fine-leafed eucalyptus tree leaning into the canyon and filled with tiny twittering birds. I looked out the other window at a glimpse of the bay when the wind parted the trees. There *must* be something I could write about. The cat, always interested in what I was doing, jumped up on the table and sat on my typing paper. Could I write about Kitty? He had a charming way of walking along the top of the picket fence to sniff the Shasta daisies, but children demanded stories. A daisy-sniffing cat would not interest them. I thought about the usual first book about a maturing of a young girl. This did not inspire me. I chewed a pencil, watched the birds, thought about how stupid I had been all those years when I aspired to write without giving a thought to what I wanted to say, petted the cat, who decided he wanted to go out. I let him out and sat down at the typewriter once more. The cat wanted in. I let him in, held him on my lap, petted him, and found myself thinking of the procession of nonreading boys who had come to the library once a week when I was a children's librarian, boys who wanted books about "kids like us."

Why not write an easy-reading book for kids like them? Good idea! All I needed was a story. How was I going to pull a story about boys from my imagination when I had spent so much of my childhood reading or embroidering? I recalled the Hancock Street neighborhood in Portland where I had lived when I was the age of the Yakima boys, a neighborhood where boys teased girls even though they played with them, where boys built scooters out of roller skates and apple boxes, wooden in those days, and where dogs, before the advent of leash laws, followed the children to school.

These musings were interrupted by a memory that sprang from my days at the hospital. A harried office worker whose husband was overseas asked if her two children, a well-behaved boy and girl, could come to the library after school. I agreed. Once they brought their dog with them, which pleased men who missed their own dogs. The next day their mother told me that a neighbor had driven the children and their dog to the hospital. When the family started home, they learned a dog was not allowed on a streetcar unless it was in a box. Rain was pouring down, the nearest grocery store that might have a box was several blocks away—by the time the woman finished her tale, she looked even more harried than usual.

Aha, I thought, the germ of a plot just right for little boys. The trouble was, I soon discovered, I did not know how to write a story. It had been thirteen years since I had written anything but letters, radio talks, and tiresome papers with footnotes. Although I had received excellent grades and complimentary comments on both high school and junior college writing, the only corrections were on spelling, punctuation, and syntax, the sort of thing dear to English teachers.

No teacher ever told me how I could improve my stories or suggested any changes at all.

If, in the 1940s, there had been writers' groups, I probably would have joined one. Fortunately, they did not exist, or if they did, I did not know about them. I believe a writer's work should spring from one person's imagination, unassisted by a group of friends who may be helpful but who also may be of questionable judgment.

As I sat listening to twittering in the eucalyptus tree and thinking of the boys from St. Joseph's, my story-hour audiences, and classes I had visited, it occurred to me that even though I was uncertain about writing, I knew how to tell a story. What was writing for children but written storytelling? So in my imagination I stood once more before Yakima's story-hour crowd as I typed the first sentence: "Henry Huggins was in the third grade." Where Henry's name came from I do not know. It was just there, waiting to be written, but I do know Henry was inspired by the boys on Hancock Street, who seemed eager to jump onto the page. Hancock Street became Klickitat Street because I had always liked the sound of the name when I had lived nearby. I moved Claudine's house from Thirty-seventh Street to renamed Hancock Street to become Henry's house. When I came to the skinny dog who found Henry, I needed a name. We happened to have spareribs waiting in the refrigerator, so I named the dog Spareribs and continued the story, based on the family who took their dog home on a streetcar. I changed the family to one boy, and the streetcar into a bus.

Writing without research, bibliography, or footnotes was a pleasure. So was rearranging life. If I needed a character or incident, all I had to do was pull it out of my memory or imagination without searching a card catalog or waiting in a crowd of pressured students at a circulation desk. What freedom!

When I finished the story I thought I was pleased with it, but I was not sure anyone else would be, so I invited a bookstore friend, Sara, who was both knowledgeable and sardonic about children's books, to come to dinner and read my story. I knew she would not try to meddle with it, and she would be honest. While I tossed the salad, Sara read "Spareribs and Henry" and gave her opinion in her no-nonsense way: "They'll be glad to get it." That was her only comment, but it gave me the assurance I needed and was the last time I asked anyone other than Clarence to read a manuscript.

What to do next? I doubted that Elisabeth Hamilton would be interested in such a slight story. To inquire about publishers I wrote to Siri Andrews, who by then had left the University of Washington to become children's editor at Holt and then librarian in Concord, New Hampshire. She suggested Abingdon-Cokesbury Press, and I sent my story on its way. As I walked down the steps of the post office, I found I was having more ideas about Henry.

The story quickly came back semirejected. The editor wrote saying, "I enjoyed reading this story very much—which is something I cannot say of all the manuscripts that come in here! It has humor, action, and realism, and I think that both boys and girls, but particularly boys from eight to eleven or so, would enjoy reading it very much." She went on to point out that a short story for this age group did not work into book format easily except as one of a collection of short stories and that this age group preferred a book-length story. She was kind enough to say that perhaps I could write a number of these "short incident" stories and submit them to magazines. "Then perhaps you could weave these stories about a plot which would carry its own suspense and climax and have a book-length manuscript to offer." If this worked out, she hoped I would send the manuscript to her, for "it seems to me it might very well fit into our publishing program."

Well! I reread the letter half a dozen times, and went to work telling/writing my other stories about Henry, which had an assortment of inspirations. One story, "The Green Christmas," was a new version of a story I had written when I was a freshman in high school, a story based on a newspaper clipping about some boys who had gone swimming downriver from a dye works that had dumped dye into the river. The boys had come out dyed green. In my high school story I had the accident save a boy from playing the part of an angel in a Christmas pageant. This turned into a story about Henry trying to get out of playing the part of a little boy in a school PTA program. (I had once been a tin soldier in such a play.) He was saved when green paint was dumped on him when he helped paint scenery.

Another chapter was based on an incident that happened to the boy next door when I lived on Thirty-seventh Street. He was passing a football to another boy across the street when a car came speeding around the corner. The football flew into the car and was never seen again—a good beginning for a story but not a satisfactory ending. Of course the boy who owned the football blamed Henry and demanded his football back. How? I recalled a summer vacation during college when some friends were talking about catching night crawlers to use for bait on a fishing trip. When I said I had never heard of night crawlers, we went on a hunting expedition. Armed with flashlights and two quart jars, we went to dimly lit Grant Park, where the lawn was damp from recent watering. In a short time we pulled from the grass two quarts of writhing worms each eight or nine inches long, a disgusting sight. Having caught them, we felt they should serve some useful purpose. What to do with two quarts of worms? "Waste not, want not," we were often reminded during the Depression.

Someone had an inspiration—we drove to a fire station that had a large fishpond. We dumped our worms into the water, which was instantly full of churning, leaping, apparently grateful fish. This incident helped me solve Henry's problems. He caught, with the help of his parents, enough night crawlers to sell to neighborhood fishermen to pay for the football. Today, in my old neighborhood, I see childish signs that say: NIGHT CRAWLERS FOR SALE.

I continued to work, combining my writing with bird-watching, letting the cat in and out, and an added activity, bread baking. After Clarence drove down the hill to the university, I often mixed a batch of bread and set it to rise over the pilot light on the gas stove. Then I sat down at the kitchen table to battle my typewriter. About the time I was ready to stretch my legs, the bread had risen, filling the house with yeasty fragrance, ready to be punched down and divided into loaves to rise again. On my next leg stretch, I put the bread in to bake and inhaled the lovely fragrance. By the time the bread was done, the cat felt neglected and sat on my paper. I pushed him off, took the bread out of the oven, buttered the crisp brown crust, and stopped writing for the day.

Hannah's company and her garden made a soothing change after a morning with my enemy the typewriter, an enemy I finally abandoned for first drafts. Ideas flowed much more easily in longhand. I continued happily inventing stories about Henry from reality and imagination, and as I wrote, Mother's words, whenever I had to write a composition in high school, came back to me: "Make it funny. People always like to read something funny," and "Keep it simple. The best writing is simple writing." Some of Professor Lehman's words also echoed through my mind: "The minutiae of life," and "The proper subject of the novel is universal human experience." I remembered Mr. Palmer's three-hundred-words-a-day assignment and disciplined myself to write every day.

Then one morning as I wrote, it occurred to

me that all the children in the stories were only children. Someone should have a sibling, so I tossed in a little sister to explain Beezus's nickname. When it came time to name the sister, I overheard a neighbor call out to another whose name was Ramona. I wrote in "Ramona," made several references to her, gave her one brief scene, and thought that was the end of her. Little did I dream, to use a trite expression from books of my childhood, that she would take over books of her own, that she would grow and become a well-known and loved character.

The group of short stories needed one last chapter. I mulled over my childhood on Hancock Street, and for some reason recalled circus posters along Sandy Boulevard when the circus was coming to town. Why not have Spareribs be a lost circus dog? I did not much like the idea, but it was all I could come up with. More mulling did not help, so that was the way I ended the book. I was not really satisfied with that last chapter. Having a clown turn up on Klickitat Street could hardly be called universal human experience, at least not in Portland, but since I had never written anything longer than those twenty-four pages on "Plato: Teacher and Theorist," the seventy or eighty pages I had written about Henry seemed as long as the novels I had studied at Cal.

What was the next step? I knew from bookstore talk and conversations at Quail's house that I was under no obligation to Abingdon-Cokesbury because the editor had not sent a contract. While I was grateful for her words of encouragement, I felt I should try a larger publisher. I thought of Elisabeth Hamilton in her handsome hat and liked the idea of my manuscripts in the hands of someone I could visualize. I also recalled that she wrote a letter when she rejected a manuscript if she felt it revealed the author showed talent.

Unfortunately, I had some reservations about Morrow as a publisher because I had met the West Coast rep several times at Quail's house and heard him express his dislike of children's books and how unnecessary he thought they were. On the other hand, at one of Quail's parties I had also heard two Morrow adult authors, Harvey Fergusson and Oregon author H. L. Davis, agree that Morrow was fair to authors. That is what I wanted, a publisher who was fair to authors. They also said that, although the rep had made much of being a talent scout, his strong point was getting books into bookstores. I could understand this because I had watched him selling to Quail at Sather Gate, where he was always kind, gentlemanly, and knowledgeable about the books on his list. I liked him; I just didn't like

his attitude toward children's books, which, however, I decided to overlook. After all, he had been
denied the experience of working with Yakima's
nonreaders, so how could he understand?

I also heard H. L. Davis remark that when he
sold his first manuscript he had walked through
the middle door of the post office when he mailed
it. He felt this had brought him luck, and ever
afterward he had walked through the middle
door of the post office whenever he mailed a
manuscript. What worked for a Pulitzer Prize-
winning author might work for me, even though
I was uneasy about that last chapter. I sent my
manuscript to Elisabeth Hamilton with my
maiden name as author and my married name
and address typed on the title page but without
a covering letter. What could I say except the
obvious: I hope you buy my book.

I had often heard Quail tell would-be authors
that if a publisher did not report on a manuscript
within six weeks, sending a letter of inquiry was
acceptable. Morrow, kind to authors, thoughtfully
sent a postcard saying my manuscript had been
received, so at least I knew it wasn't lost in the
mail. After several weeks went by, I began to
watch for the mailman while clipping off dead
roses to disguise my true purpose. Since he had
never seen me in the garden, he became curious

and wanted to know what I was waiting for. When I explained, he began to watch for my mail as eagerly as I, and at the end of six weeks, left his heavy mailbag by the hedge and came running down the steps waving an airmail letter. "It's here!" he shouted as I ran to meet him. A letter, not a returned manuscript! I went into the house to read it.

I tore open the envelope and read the first sentence of Elisabeth Hamilton's letter dated July 25, 1949. "Several of us have read your story, 'Spareribs and Henry,' and we are very much interested in it as a possibility for the Morrow list." She went on to praise the story and to say that "the last chapter, 'Finders Keepers,' was not up to the previous chapters." How right she was. She then asked if I would be willing to make revisions. Of course I would, in my own blood, if necessary. She closed by saying she was going on vacation until shortly after the middle of August, and if I would undertake revisions, she would send criticisms and suggestions on her return. I flopped into a chair and, smiling at the whole world, read and reread the letter. Then I telephoned Clarence to give him the news and wrote a letter saying I would be pleased to make revisions.

The middle of August, I started pulling weeds

in the garden, but this time confessed to the mailman my motive, other than getting rid of weeds. "Not today," he said every day until the middle of September, when I had pulled a lot of weeds. He ran down the steps once more, this time waving a big brown envelope, as pleased as if he were giving me a personal gift. I tore it open and read Mrs. Hamilton's first paragraph, which concluded with: ". . . my ideas of what I hope you will do with it are very definite indeed." That sentence had a do-it-or-else ring.

The suggestions began, "1. Is it important to you to use the pen name Beverly Bunn? We all like Beverly B. Cleary better." This gave me pause. I liked my maiden name because it was a name people remembered. I finally agreed to the change provided the middle initial was dropped, an initial that had been foisted on me by the U.S. Government even though my middle name was Atlee. When I wrote home, Mother was indignant. "Bunn is a fine old pioneer name," she wrote. A number of books later, Elisabeth, as I called Mrs. Hamilton by then, apologized for being so presumptuous.

Mrs. Hamilton also disliked the dog's name and suggested Ribs or Ribsy as sounding more like one a boy would choose. She was right. Why couldn't I have seen that? Then came her most valuable suggestions: "There are several highly dramatic spots in the story, which should be developed better. These incidents are now described very briefly, and the value of the story is partly thrown away." She listed five sentences, all of them easy to expand. And then there was the last chapter. Mrs. Hamilton was blunt: "We don't like the last chapter at all." She went on to say it could be left out altogether; on the other hand, parts were too good to drop. "The circus idea is so threadbare that I would much prefer to have no reference to a circus at all in the story." She was right, and I have recalled this sentence many times over the years whenever I see another circus story or toy. Mrs. Hamilton went on to say I could make the dog's former owner an ordinary person and develop the best parts of the chapter. She closed by saying that the book would probably be priced at $2.00 and they could offer 8 percent on the first 10,000 copies and 10 percent thereafter, with an advance against royalties of $500. If I would agree with the suggestions, she would have a contract drawn up. I was so naïve I hadn't known how many details a contract would cover.

After I had studied Mrs. Hamilton's suggestions, I saw that they actually involved very little work. They were easily made and sent off; a contract and check arrived, as well as a letter saying, "We all think this is going to be one of the exciting publications of the fall." The book was now titled *Henry Huggins*. After all my years of ambition to write, of aiming both consciously and unconsciously toward writing, I had actually written. I was a real live author. I was most grateful to Elisabeth Hamilton for the first instruction in writing fiction I had ever received.

I telephoned the bookstore to tell Sara, who spread the news. Then I told other friends. Everyone was surprised and congratulated me with varying degrees of enthusiasm. One neighbor said, "I think it's just great that you sat quietly at home and cracked that New York crowd. *Now* you can be eccentric." Harvey Fergusson said, "Why don't you quit fooling around with children's books and write for adults? I have a hunch you could write like Katherine Mansfield." Hannah was pleased for me, but she was also indignant because I had not given my manuscript to the Morrow rep to submit for me. "Don't you want to be a feather in his cap?" she asked. No, I didn't want to be a feather in anyone's cap, especially the cap of a man who had so vigorously expressed a dislike for children's books. The rep, the next time he was in Berkeley, said, "Don't go out and buy a yacht, but this book will sell." He did very well by it, and so did Sather Gate because Quail offered it to every customer who came in. She sold five hundred copies during the Christmas rush of 1950. Mother wrote that Dad was proud of me and that she was telephoning everyone with the news. Clarence said he knew all along I could do it.

After keeping the advance royalty check for a few days to admire, I took it to the bank to deposit. As I walked down the winding road, the sky shone blue through the gray-green eucalyptus leaves, but because eucalyptus buds tend to roll underfoot, I watched my step. Half-hidden by a sickle-shaped leaf was a nickel. I picked it up and put it in my pocket, and as I walked, my fingers played with that worn nickel while my mental pump, having been primed by *Henry Huggins,* was at work on a story about a girl named Ellen Tebbits who had trouble hiding her woolen underwear at ballet class.

I was confident that a satisfying life of writing lay ahead, that ideas would continue to flow. As I walked, I thought about all the bits of knowledge about children, reading, and writing that had clung to me like burrs or dandelion fluff all through childhood, college, the Yakima children's room, and the bookstore. As I mulled over my past, I made two resolutions: I would ignore all trends, and I would not let money influence any decisions I would make about my books.

I was so happy, the day was so bright and fragrant, that I did not bother to take the bus at the bottom of the hill but walked on down Euclid Avenue, across the campus, past buildings where I had attended classes, the building that brought painful memories of the English Comprehensive, the library where I had spent so many evenings with Clarence, the Sather Gate Book Shop, to the bank next door. There I deposited the check and one worn nickel for luck.

In my years of writing I have often thought of that nickel and now see it as a talisman of all the good fortune that has come to me: friends, readers, awards, travel, children of my own, financial security that has allowed me to return the generosity extended to me when times were hard for everyone. It was indeed a lucky nickel.